FUNERARY PRACTICES IN THE NETHERLANDS

Funerary International Series

Series Editor: Julie Rugg, University of York, UK

The study of mortality is now an established academic endeavour which is rapidly expanding in scale and in disciplinary reach. One missing element is a repository of basic facts about funerary practice in each country and the broader legal, governance and denominational frameworks for those practices which might serve to set more detailed research in context.

This book series remedies this absence by producing country-specific monographs, with texts providing a standard framework of questions, which ensures even coverage, aids international comparison, fosters international linkages across the academic community and inspires new research directions. These texts will be a valuable resource for researchers across the humanities and social sciences concerned with death and funerary customs.

Previous titles in this series

Julie Rugg and Brian Parsons, *Funerary Practices in England and Wales*

Forthcoming in this series

Olga Nešporová, *Funerary Practices in the Czech Republic*
Christoph Streb, *Funerary Practices in Germany*
Aleksandra Pavićević, *Funerary Practices in Serbia*
Maija Butters and Ilona Pajari, *Funerary Practices in Finland*

FUNERARY PRACTICES IN THE NETHERLANDS

BY

BRENDA MATHIJSSEN
University of Groningen, The Netherlands

CLAUDIA VENHORST
Radboud University Nijmegen, The Netherlands

emerald
PUBLISHING

United Kingdom – North America – Japan
India – Malaysia – China

Emerald Publishing Limited
Howard House, Wagon Lane, Bingley BD16 1WA, UK

First edition 2019

Reprints and permissions service
Contact: permissions@emeraldinsight.com

British Library Cataloguing in Publication Data
A catalogue record for this book is available from the British Library

ISBN: 978-1-78769-876-5 (Print)
ISBN: 978-1-78769-873-4 (Online)
ISBN: 978-1-78769-875-8 (Epub)

INVESTOR IN PEOPLE

CONTENTS

List of Images xi

List of Tables and Charts xv

Preface xvii

Acknowledgements xix

Map of The Netherlands xxi

1. The Netherlands: An Introduction 1
   - 1.1. Overview 1
   - 1.2. Pillars and Polders 2
   - 1.3. Migration and Diversity 3
   - 1.4. Religion in Numbers 6
2. History 9
   - 2.1. The Sixteenth and Seventeenth Centuries 9
   - 2.2. The Eighteenth and Nineteenth Centuries 12
   - 2.3. The Early Twentieth Century 17
   - 2.4. The Late Twentieth Century 19
3. Demographic and Legal Frameworks 23
   - 3.1. Mortality in the Netherlands 23
     - 3.1.1. Place of Death 24
     - 3.1.2. Causes of Death 24
   - 3.2. Legal Frameworks 24
     - 3.2.1. The Euthanasia Act 25
     - 3.2.2. Corpse Disposal Act 26

3.3. Recent Developments in Legislation 34
3.3.1. Resomation, Cryomation and Compostation 35
3.3.2. Changes in the Personal Records Database 36
3.3.3. Recent Jurisprudence 37

4. The Funeral Directing Industry 39
4.1. Historic Development 39
4.2. Current Organisation 41
4.2.1. Types of Funeral Organisations 42
4.2.2. Trade Associations 45
4.2.3. Education and Quality Management 47
4.2.4. Typical Premises of the Funeral Home 48
4.3. Contemporary Developments: Gender, Diversity and Heritage 50
4.3.1. The Female Face of Death 50
4.3.2. A Multicultural Funeral Home 52
4.3.3. Reallocating Religious Heritage 53
4.4. Public Appearances: Televised Funeral Commercials 54

5. Paying for Funerals 57
5.1. Average Funeral Costs 57
5.2. Breakdown of General, Burial and Cremation Costs 58
5.3. Types of Funeral Insurance 59
5.4. Funeral Poverty and Municipal Help 62
5.5. Special Income Support 63
5.6. Technical Cremation 64
5.7. Baby and Children's Funerals 65

6. A Typical Funeral 67
6.1. Diverse and Tailor-made Funerals 67
6.2. Immediately Following Death 68
6.3. Making Funeral Arrangements 70
6.3.1. Advance Funeral Wishes 71
6.3.2. The Lonely Funeral: A Poetic Initiative 73
6.4. Arrangements with the Funeral Director 74
6.4.1. Type of Funeral 74
6.4.2. Place, Time and Length of the Service 74
6.4.3. Mourning Cards and Death Notices 75

6.4.4. The Coffin or Shroud 75
6.4.5. Flowers 77
6.4.6. Music 78
6.4.7. Koffietafel 79
6.5. Arrangements with the Religious or Civil Celebrant 79
6.5.1. Minister, Pastor or Priest 80
6.5.2. Imam and Volunteers 81
6.5.3. Chevra Kadisha 82
6.5.4. Pandit 83
6.5.5. Humanistic Celebrant 83
6.5.6. Ritual Coach or Civil Celebrant 84
6.6. The Care of the Deceased 84
6.6.1. Ritual Washing 87
6.6.2. Viewing the Deceased 87
6.7. The Day of the Funeral 89
6.7.1. Dress 89
6.7.2. Travel to the Funeral Service 89
6.7.3. The Place of the Funeral 92
6.7.4. Decorating the Funeral Location 92
6.7.5. Orders of Service 93
6.7.6. Attending the Funeral 93
6.7.7. The Funeral Service 94
6.7.8. Committal, Burial and Cremation 98
6.7.9. Digital Recording 99
6.7.10. Remembrance or Prayer Cards 100
6.7.11. After the Funeral Service 103

7. Burial and Cemeteries 105
7.1. Historic Development 105
7.2. Current Cemetery Provision 107
7.2.1. Municipal Cemeteries 109
7.2.2. Special Cemeteries 112
7.3. Graves 125
7.3.1. Technicalities 126
7.3.2. Grave Rights and Terms 129
7.3.3. Clearing of Graves 130
7.3.4. Burial Costs 131

7.3.5. Grave Covers 133
7.3.6. Preservation 136
7.4. Cemetery Variation in the Netherlands 137
7.4.1. Marken and Volendam: Protestant and Catholic Traditions 138
7.4.2. Roermond: The Old Cemetery 140
7.4.3. Amsterdam: De Nieuwe Ooster 142
7.4.4. Beth Haim: Portuguese Jewish Cemetery 144
7.4.5. Syrian Orthodox Cemetery Glanerbrug 146
7.4.6. A Variety of Muslim Burial Plots 147

8. Cremation and Crematoria 151
8.1. Historic Development 151
8.2. Burial vs Cremation 157
8.3. Current Crematorium Provision 159
8.4. Crematorium Architecture 160
8.5. Cremation Law and Certification 162
8.5.1. Current Legal Debates 164
8.6. Crematorium Logistics 166
8.6.1. Welcoming Facilities at the Crematorium 167
8.6.2. Cremation Services in the Auditorium 168
8.6.3. Crematoria and Funeral Music 171
8.6.4. Incineration and the Witnessing of the Charge 171
8.6.5. The Crematorium Bar and Restaurant 174
8.6.6. The Technical Cremation Process 174
8.6.7. Environmental Regulations 175
8.6.8. Cremulation and Ash Storage 178
8.7. The Ashes 178
8.7.1. Retrieving the Ashes 178
8.7.2. Types of Ash Disposal 180
8.7.3. Ash Artists and Entrepreneurs 181
8.7.4. Accommodating Hindu Ash Disposal 183
8.8. Cremation Equipment and OrthoMetals 184

9. Death and Remembrance in the Public Sphere 187
9.1. Personal Commemoration: Between Private and Public 187
9.1.1. All Souls' Day 188
9.1.2. Virtual Commemoration 190
9.2. War and Holocaust Commemoration 191
9.2.1. National Remembrance of the Dead: May 4 191
9.2.2. Holocaust Names Memorial 192
9.2.3. Honour Fields and War Cemeteries 193
9.2.4. German Military Cemetery Ysselsteyn 195
9.3. Notable Developments in Dutch Memorial Practices 196
9.3.1. Spontaneous Commemorations 196
9.3.2. Dying Publicly 197
9.3.3. MH17: Public Mourning 199

Bibliography 201

Index 209

LIST OF IMAGES

Chapter 2

Image 2.1. Code of the Funeral Association *Tot Aller Welzijn* ('For Everyone's Wellbeing'). . . . 14

Image 2.2. Image of the Westerveld Crematorium in Driehuis-Velsen in 1913, the Year of Its Opening. 18

Chapter 4

Image 4.1. A Small Auditorium in a Funeral Home in Overasselt, Gelderland. 50

Chapter 6

Image 6.1. An Example of a Contemporary Mourning Card, with Fictional Information, Based on Digital Templates. 76

Image 6.2. A Hearse, Characterised by the Triangular Flags with Three White Stripes at the Front. 90

Image 6.3. A Funeral Bicycle, Used to Transport the Deceased to the Cemetery or Crematorium. 91

Image 6.4. Religious Symbols at a Dutch Crematorium. 93

Image 6.5. Typical Mourning Card 1951. 101
Image 6.6. Typical Modern Mourning Card 2014. . 102

Chapter 7

Image 7.1. Grave Candle Vending Machine at Rustoord Cemetery in Nijmegen, Gelderland. 112
Image 7.2. Roman Catholic Cemetery in Nijmegen, Gelderland. 114
Image 7.3. The Old Cemetery in Sauwerd, Groningen, with Protestant Headstones.. 117
Image 7.4. Jewish Cemetery in Dwingeloo, Drenthe. 119
Image 7.5. Muslim Burial Site, Grave Plots at Municipal Cemetery Blerickse Bergen in Venlo, Limburg. 120
Image 7.6. Grave at a Natural Burial Ground in Blerick/Maasbree, Limburg. 123
Image 7.7. Open Air Auditorium at Natural Burial Ground in Blerick/Maasbree, Limburg. . 124
Image 7.8. Canadian War Cemetery and Memorial in Groesbeek, Gelderland. 124
Image 7.9. 'You are the sweetest dog'. A Memorial Plaque at the Pet Cemetery in Grashoek, Limburg.. 125
Image 7.10. Overview of a Burial Plot at Municipal Cemetery Venlo, Limburg, with New Graves. 127
Image 7.11. Open Spaces at the Cemetery after Grave Plot Clearance. 131

Image 7.12. Esserveld Cemetery, Groningen: The Most Expensive Cemetery in the Netherlands. 132
Image 7.13. Balloon-decorated Grave to Celebrate the Deceased's Birthday. 135
Image 7.14. Protestant Cemetery of Marken, Noord Holland. 139
Image 7.15. Roman Catholic Cemetery of Volendam, Noord Holland. 139
Image 7.16. Grave with the Hands at the Old Cemetery in Roermond, Limburg. 141
Image 7.17. An Elaborately Decorated Seventeenth-century Grave at the Portuguese Jewish Cemetery Beth Haim in Ouderkerk aan de Amstel, Noord Holland. 146
Image 7.18. A Recent Grave at the Portuguese Jewish Cemetery Beth Haim in Ouderkerk aan de Amstel, Noord Holland. 147
Image 7.19. Children's Grave at the Muslim Cemetery in Venlo-Blerick, Limburg. 149

Chapter 8

Image 8.1. Early Twentieth-century Cremation Propaganda of the *Vereeniging voor Facultatieve Lijkverbranding*. 154
Image 8.2. A Building Plan of the Westerveld Crematorium. 155
Image 8.3. The Leiden Murderess Maria Catharina Swanenburg. 165

Image 8.4. Small Auditorium at a Crematorium in Gelderland. 170
Image 8.5. Witnessing the Charge of the Deceased at a Crematorium in Gelderland. 173
Image 8.6. The Technical Cremation Process: The Operator Removes the Cremated Remains. 176
Image 8.7. The Technical Cremation Process: After Cremulation the Ashes Are Placed in Ash Containers for Storage.. 177
Image 8.8. The Ash Storage Room. 179
Image 8.9. Ash Scattering Garden at Crematorium Blerick, Limburg. 182
Image 8.10. Buckets Collecting Ortho Materials for Recycling. 185

Chapter 9

Image 9.1. A Commemoration Tree at an All Souls' Event. 190

LIST OF TABLES AND CHARTS

Chapter 1

Table 1.1. Migration in the Netherlands, 2018. 7

Table 1.2. Religious Affiliation in the Netherlands: Historical Development, 1830–2015. . . . 8

Chapter 4

Chart 4.1. Number of Funeral Companies and Employees in 2007 and 2019. 42

Chapter 5

Table 5.1. Average Funeral Costs.. 59

Table 5.2. Average Burial Costs. 60

Table 5.3. Average Cremation Costs. 60

Chapter 6

Table 6.1. Place of Death. 68

Chapter 8

Table 8.1. Development of Cremation in the Netherlands. 158

Table 8.2. Number of Crematoria in the Netherlands. . 160

PREFACE

Death is inevitable to each of us and to those we hold dear. It is a matter of existential concern. People's experiences with death are highly diverse, and so are their funerary practices. They are influenced by regional customs, legal frameworks and personal preferences. Moreover, our responses to loss are shaped by our age, ethnicity, class, gender and religion, as well as by the type and time of a death, and our relationship to the deceased.

People's varied experiences with death challenge researchers who want to study funerary repertoires. How does one describe a miscellaneous field of practices, beliefs and experiences? How can one grasp its changes over time? Many researchers, including us, solve this difficulty by bypassing it. We situate our specific (Dutch) context in a larger, seemingly homogeneous one: Europe or the West. Rather than unpicking the notion of 'Western' death practices and its political implications, we have created a myth of Western funerary culture.

In the writing and structuring of this book, the notion of Western death ways proved problematic. It has, for instance, been impossible to translate some funerary practices and legislations to a (partially) non-Dutch and English-speaking audience, without compromising on the cultural aspects and meanings. At many occasions we discussed whether we should refer to the 'Dutch Burial and Cremation Act' or the

'Corpse Disposal Act', and whether we should speak of autopsies and sections while the Dutch word *lijkschouwing* clearly indicates that the coroner primarily observes the corpse, rather than dissecting it.

The Funerary International Series provides accessible information on funerary practices in different (European) countries, and thereby aims to modestly unpick the notion of 'Western' funerary culture. This book does so for the Netherlands. It provides a concise introduction to contemporary funerary practices, and their historic, geographic, demographic, (multi)cultural and political context.

Although we have made a selection of funerary practices, as well as some simplifications to provide a clear and manageable overview, we want to emphasise the dynamics of funerary practices and the diversity of society. The Dutch funerary landscapes have been shaped by a Protestant majority in the North and a Roman Catholic majority in the South, by the segregation of society in pillars, by the arrival of migrants from the former colonies of Surinam and Indonesia, and from the Caribbean territories, as well as by the arrival of guest workers and refugees from the peripheries of Europe and elsewhere, by individualisation and secularisation, by emancipation movements, and by technical innovation. Thus although 'the' Dutch funerary culture does not exist, we look forward to offering you some insight into it.

Brenda Mathijssen and Claudia Venhorst

ACKNOWLEDGEMENTS

This book has been written with the support of many. We are especially grateful to all of our research participants. Many of you have shared your personal stories of loss, of conducting funerals and of experiencing bereavement. You have taught us about funerary practices and frameworks, and more importantly, about the associated emotions, creativity and resilience. Some of you have invited us to conduct fieldwork at funeral homes, cemeteries and crematoria, and have shown what it means to work in this field. Thank you for your openness. We hope that this book resonates with your own professional experiences, and provides a useful source in your future practice.

We are also deeply indebted to our current and former colleagues at the Department of Comparative Religion and the Centre for Thanatology at Radboud University Nijmegen; the Department of Comparative Study of Religion at the University of Groningen; the Centre for Death and Life Studies at Durham University; and the Department of Human Geography at the University of Reading. We especially like to thank Eric Venbrux, Peter Nissen and Thomas Quartier for supporting us from the very start and for introducing us to the fields of Death Studies and Religious Studies. Julie, a special thanks to you for sticking to the plan of making a Funerary International Series, and for entrusting the Dutch volume to us.

Finally, our deep gratitude is extended to Philippa Grand, Sophie Darling and Rachel Ward for their support and patience throughout the writing and editing process.

MAP OF THE NETHERLANDS

CHAPTER 1

THE NETHERLANDS: AN INTRODUCTION

1.1. OVERVIEW

The Netherlands, called *Nederland* in Dutch, is a rather small and densely populated country in North Western Europe. It borders Germany at the east and Belgium to the south. The country is often (incorrectly) referred to as 'Holland', the historic name of just two of the current 12 provinces: Noord-Holland, Zuid-Holland, Utrecht, Zeeland, Brabant, Limburg, Gelderland, Overijssel, Flevoland, Drenthe, Friesland and Groningen. Within the provinces 355 municipalities can be found, forming the lowest level of governance. The municipality provides services and policy at a local level. Together with three island territories in the Caribbean (Bonaire, Saint Eustatius and Saba), these provinces make up the Kingdom of the Netherlands (see map on page xxi).

The Netherlands is a parliamentary constitutional monarchy. Its central government is seated in The Hague and Amsterdam is its capital city. It is part of the European Union, the Euro-zone and the Schengen Area. It qualifies as a welfare state which provides universal healthcare, public education, infrastructure and social benefits. *Nederland* or 'lower land' refers to the fact that more than a quarter of the country is situated below sea level, and the rest a mere metre above. The landscape is moulded by canals, rivers and lakes. The fight against water is of all times and ongoing, influencing many day-to-day practices. High groundwater levels often complicate the burying of the dead, demanding innovative and costly solutions and putting pressure on available burial space in certain areas.

With 17.2 million inhabitants on 41,500 km^2 (of which 33,700 km^2 actual land), the Netherlands is one of the most densely populated countries in the world. Well over 90% of the population is living in cities. The four largest cities – Amsterdam, Rotterdam, The Hague and Utrecht – and their surrounding areas form the so-called *Randstad* metropolis: the densely populated (8.2 million inhabitants in 2018) economic heart of the country. The mixed-market economy is among the top economies in the world, and the Netherlands is the world's second largest exporter of food and agricultural products due to intensive and innovative agriculture.

1.2. PILLARS AND POLDERS

The Netherlands was long deeply divided along religious lines. From the nineteenth century onwards, this led to a policy of pillarisation, causing and facilitating a politico-denominational segregation of society. Each segment or pillar – Protestant, Roman Catholic, Social Democratic – could clearly be differentiated by means of their own media, political parties, leisure clubs, schools, healthcare providers and funerary services. The institutional segregation emancipated the various groups and also reduced personal contacts between the members of different pillars to a minimum. The liberals who fundamentally opposed the segmentation ironically ended up in a (rather small) pillar of their own. As the government accommodated the pillarised system, they also (probably unintentionally) helped to emancipate the working and lower middle classes from elite control.

The particular experience of the Second World War – the Dutch stayed neutral during the First World War, and the last 'war' they were involved with was the so-called Ten Day's Campaign against Belgium in 1831 – instigated a desire to renew the political system and break down the segmentation. The process of 'depillarisation' began, and turned on steam from the 1960s onwards. Today remnants of the former policy are still visible, particularly in the media and in education. Public television, for example, is organised through pillarised broadcasting companies, as are several newspapers. Also, the historic patchwork of political parties and the consequent multiple party coalition governments has become common practice in the Netherlands. The desire to break down the segmentation has also grounded the Dutch socio-economic model of consensus decision-making, the so-called *poldermodel*, common good throughout the 1980s and 1990s.

1.3. MIGRATION AND DIVERSITY

In the second half of the twentieth century, the Netherlands further diversified. As the pillars crumbled, church membership dropped and individualisation processes accelerated. Moreover, a variety of religious and cultural groups arrived in the Netherlands, for example, through guest worker programmes or after the dismantling of colonial administrative services, for example, in Indonesia. These migrants brought with them a variety of customs and practices, including funeral repertoires that had to be reinvented in view of this new context, where they found themselves in a minority position.

Migration has always been part of Dutch history.[1] Immigration spiked from the sixteenth century onwards, when tens of thousands of Protestants (from the Southern Netherlands and elsewhere in Europe) found a safe haven in the Northern Netherlands. Portuguese and Spanish Jews, fleeing the Spanish inquisition, were followed by German- or Yiddish-speaking Jews and French Huguenots in the seventeenth century. These were highly prosperous times in the Netherlands, making it attractive for large numbers of labour migrants from (what is now) Germany and Eastern Europe. Emigration was rather low. Certain Protestant groups, like the Mennonites, were in open conflict with the rather strict Calvinists and searched for a new home elsewhere. Sailors and soldiers were recruited to support the trade activities of the Dutch West India Company, a company that was instrumental in the short-lived Dutch colonisation of the Americas, and the Dutch East India Company that developed commercial and industrial activities in South East Asia.

Whereas there was little immigration in the nineteenth century, numbers gradually increased in the twentieth century as people became richer, travel became faster and more affordable, and international trade expanded. Between 1946 and 1963 about 400,000 people arrived from the Dutch East Indies, as they were unable to stay after the proclamation of Indonesian Independence in 1945 and its recognition by the

[1]For detailed information on five centuries of migration to and from the Netherlands: Obdeijn, H., & Schrover, M. (2008). *Komen en gaan. Immigratie en emigratie in Nederland vanaf 1550*. Amsterdam: Uitgeverij Bert Bakker.

Dutch government and the UN in 1949.[2] At about the same time, about half a million people left the Netherlands to find a better (and safer) future in Canada and Australia, but also in New Zealand, South Africa, Brazil and the United States. Between 1960 and 1974, 150,000 'guest workers', mainly from Turkey and Morocco, were recruited for industrial labour to support the rapidly growing Dutch economy.[3] Due to family reunification their number continued to increase after 1974.

In anticipation of the independence of Surinam in 1975, many – mainly Hindustani and Javanese – migrated to the Netherlands. Inhabitants of Suriname and the Dutch Antilles were granted Dutch nationality in 1954 and were free to relocate within the Dutch Kingdom. Also after independence large numbers of Surinamese (predominantly Afro-Surinamese) continued to immigrate to attend higher education and to reunite with family. Today, Suriname has a population of 556,485 and 351,681 people of Suriname descent are living in the Netherlands.[4]

From the 1990s onwards, war and famine caused a rising number of refugees to settle in the Netherlands, for example, from (former) Yugoslavia, Congo, Sri Lanka, Afghanistan, Iraq, Somalia and more recently from Syria.[5] They do share migration motives and experiences but are of diverse national, cultural and religious backgrounds. In 2018, 23% of the Dutch population has a so-called migration

---

[2]Obdeijn and Schrover (2008), pp. 229–248.

[3]Obdeijn and Schrover (2008), p. 284.

[4]Obdeijn and Schrover (2008), p. 255; CBS. (2018). Retrieved from https://statline.cbs.nl/Statweb/publication/?DM=SLNL&PA=71090NED&D1=0&D2=0&D3=0&D4=7&D5=1-2&D6=96%2c108&VW=T

[5]Obdeijn and Schrover (2008), p. 328.

background (see Table 1.1).[6] The migration balance – the number of people who settled in the Netherlands minus residents who left the Netherlands to settle elsewhere – was 80,665 in 2017.

1.4. RELIGION IN NUMBERS

In 2015, Statistics Netherlands (CBS) found that 50.1% of the adult population declared to be not religiously affiliated. Christians comprised 43.8% of the total population and were divided between Catholics with 23.7% and the members of the Protestant Church of the Netherlands with 15.5%, members of other Christian denominations were 4.6%. Muslims comprised 4.9% of the total population, Hindus 0.6%, Buddhists 0.4% and Jews 0.1% (see Table 1.2).[7]

As Dutch society has become super-diverse, a wide variety of ideas and practices have emerged both in- and outside religious and ideological movements. These include 'new' perspectives on dying, death and grief. People actively look for funerary practices that suit the current time and circumstances.

[6]Retrieved from https://www.cbs.nl/en-gb/background/2018/47/population. Accessed on March 30, 2019; the CBS defines a person with a migration background as a 'person of whom at least one parent was born abroad. A distinction is made between persons born abroad (first-generation) and persons born in the Netherlands (second-generation)'. See https://www.cbs.nl/en-gb/our-services/methods/definitions?tab=p#id=person-with-a-migration-background. Accessed on March 30, 2019.

[7]Schmeets, H. (2016). *De religieuze kaart van Nederland, 2010-2015*. Centraal Bureau voor de Statistiek. Retrieved from https://www.cbs.nl/nl-nl/publicatie/2016/51/de-religieuze-kaart-van-nederland-2010-2015.

Table 1.1. Migration in the Netherlands, 2018.

	Migration Background[a]	First Generation	Second Generation
Total population	17,181,084		
With migration background	3,971,859	2,079,329	1,892,530
Western[b]	1,729,016	836,178	892,838
Non-Western[c]	2,242,843	1,243,151	999,692
Country of origin			
Turkey	404,459	191,513	212,946
Morocco	396,539	169,018	227,521
Indonesia	361,594	100,922	260,672
Germany	354,136	105,355	248,781
Surinam	351,681	176,412	175,269
Belgium	118,725	45,492	73,233
Poland	173,050	134,999	38,051
United Kingdom	88,390	49,358	39,032
Iraq	61,255	43,864	17,391
Italy	53,703	31,375	22,328

Sources: CBS. (2019). *Population and population dynamics by month, 1995-2018.* Retrieved from https://opendata.cbs.nl/statline/#/CBS/en/dataset/37943eng/table?dl=1ECD4; CBS. (2019). *Immi- en emigratie; leeftijd (31 dec.), burgerlijke staat, geboorteland.* Retrieved from https://opendata.cbs.nl/#/CBS/nl/dataset/03742/table?ts=1554047997040

Notes: [a]Migration background refers to the country with which a person has the closest ties, based on his/her parents' country of birth or his/her own country of birth. [b]Person originating from a country in Europe (excluding Turkey), North America and Oceania, or from Indonesia or Japan. [c]Person originating from a country in Africa, South America or Asia (excl. Indonesia and Japan) or from Turkey.

Table 1.2. Religious Affiliation in the Netherlands: Historical Development, 1830–2015.

Year	Protestants[a]	Roman Catholics	Jews	Muslims	Other Christians/ Other Denominations	No Religious Affiliation
1830	59.1	40.8	1.8	–	0.1	–
1869	61.3	36.6	1.9	–	0.1	–
1899	60.0	35.3	2.0	–	0.4	2.3
1920	53.8	35.8	1.7	–	1.0	7.8
1930	46.3	36.5	1.4	–	1.4	14.4
1947	42.3	38.6	0.1	–	1.9	17.1
1960	40.7	40.5	0.1	0.0	0.2	18.3
1971	35.9	40.5	0.1	0.4	0.3	23.6
1980	30	38	–	1.7[b]	5	26
1990	26	33	–	3.1[b]	6	38
2000	21	32	–	4.4[b]	8	40
2010	17.9	27.3	0.1	4.5	5.1	45.3
2015	15.5	23.7	0.1	4.9	5.6	50.1

Sources: Schmeets, H. (2016). *De religieuze kaart van Nederland, 2010-2015*. Den Haag: Centraal Bureau voor de Statistiek. Retrieved from https://www.cbs.nl/nl-nl/publicatie/2016/51/de-religieuze-kaart-van-nederland-2010-2015; Volkstellingen (1795–1971), www.volkstellingen.nl; CBS. (2015). *Kerkelijke gezindte en kerkbezoek 18492017*, retrieved from https://statline.cbs.nl/Statweb/publication/?DM=SLNL&PA=37944&D1=0-5&D2=a&HDR=T&STB=G1&VW=T; Buijs, F., & Rath, J. (2002). *Muslims in Europe: The state of research. IMISCOE Working Paper.* Amsterdam: IMES; Stoffels, H. & Walinga, P. (2005). 'Ontwikkelingen in de ledenaantallen van een aantal Nederlandse kerkgenootschappen (tabel)'. In: SCP (Ed.). *De sociale staat van Nederland.* Den Haag: Sociaal en Cultureel Planbureau.
Notes: Numbers indicate percentages. [a]People identified with the Nederlands Hervormde Kerk, Gereformeerde Kerk Nederland or Protestantse Kerk Nederland; all are members of the Protestant Church in the Netherlands. [b]These estimates are based on census data focusing on migration background rather than religion. Therefore, they have limitations. In 2006, the CSB adopted a new approach to calculate religious affiliations.

CHAPTER 2

HISTORY

2.1. THE SIXTEENTH AND SEVENTEENTH CENTURIES

The Roman Catholic Church and its priests have played a dominant role in people's dealings with death and dying in the Netherlands. Over time, the Church had incorporated pre-Christian notions of death into its liturgy.[1] These notions and the associated practices had appeared to be rather persistent and difficult to change. From the fourteenth century onwards, the position of the Church itself, and especially its authoritarianism, became increasingly questioned.[2] The sixteenth and seventeenth century were tumultuous times in Europe with widespread wars fought over both political and religious issues. The Netherlands, led by Calvinists, freed themselves from Spanish (and Roman Catholic) rule. Several provinces created a confederacy in 1581 and in 1648, after the Dutch Revolt or the Eighty Years' War, the Dutch

[1]Kok, H. (2005). *Thanatos. De geschiedenis van de laatste eer.* Heeswijk-Dinther: Berne boekmakerij, 110.
[2]Oberman, H. (2003). *The two Reformations. The journey from the last days to the new world.* New Haven, CA: Yale University Press.

republic was recognised. The Dutch Reformed Church – *de Nederlandse Hervormde Kerk* – was founded in 1571.[3] Theologically it was shaped not only by John Calvin, but also by other major Protestant Reformers. Further theological developments and controversies during its history, including Arminianism, the *Nadere Reformatie* (1600–1750) and a number of splits in the nineteenth century, such as the *Doleantie* led by Abraham Kuyper, would greatly diversify Dutch Calvinism.

When the independence of the Netherlands was recognised in 1648, the country did not only contain the seven Protestant provinces of the Dutch Republic. It also included the Generality Lands (*Generaliteitslanden*), roughly the current southern provinces of North Brabant and Limburg, which remained Catholic. The country could practically be divided in a Protestant North and a Roman Catholic South, although significant Catholic enclaves have always remained in the north. The Protestants rejected Catholicism and the native Catholics, and treated them in a harsh manner. Simultaneously, however, they were tolerant towards the Jews and they took in religious dissenters from elsewhere, including other Protestants.

The Protestant North was not unified. The Dutch Reformation had spread through multiple popular movements, rather than via one reigning power, and multiple churches existed. Although never formally adopted as the state religion, the Dutch Reformed Church did enjoy the status of 'public' or 'privileged' church. Until 1795 every public

[3]The Dutch Reformed Church was founded as the *Nederduitse Gereformeerde Kerk* and was renamed the *Nederlandse Hervormde Kerk* in 1816.

official had to be a communicant member, and the Church thus had close relations with the Dutch government.

Calvinists formally restrained funeral rites. The 1618–1619 Synod of Dort prohibited the tradition of sitting vigil at a deathbed (*dodewake*), a custom among both Jews and Catholics.[4] The Synod also abolished the eulogies and the symbolic scoop of earth that relatives cast in the grave.[5] Funeral services with candlelight and church bell ringing were no longer in favour, and the Roman Catholic doctrine of Purgatory was invalidated. It was replaced by the doctrine of Predestination, according to which all events have already been ordained by God. Whom God will save and whom he will reject has been predetermined. In this regard, the deceased could no longer be 'prayed to heaven' and the absolution, the last recommendation for farewell, disappeared from Protestant funeral services. To give an indication of the number of souls that could rejoice in heaven, a quotation from the Gospel of Matthew was often used: 'For many are called, but few are chosen'.

Sober funerals, simple graves and the idea of equality in death were widely promoted by Calvinists but costly and prestigious burials in churches continued despite fierce attempts to eradicate 'papal superstitions and practices'. Not only were the already established practices difficult to change, as the Roman Catholics had experienced in the centuries before, the burials were also a welcome source of income for the churches. The Protestant Churches were less involved in the practical aspects of funerals and, unlike the Catholic

---

[4]Nissen, P. (2013). 'Words for the final hour. On deathbed prayer in the Christian tradition'. In E. Venbrux et. al. (eds.). *Changing European death ways*. Munster: Lit Verlag.

[5]Sinnema, D., Moser, C. & Selderhuis, H. (eds.). (2014). *Acta et Documenta Synodi Nationalis Dordrechtanae (1618–1619)*. Göttingen: Vandenhoeck & Ruprecht.

Priests who had provided absolution, the ministers were not part of people's deathbed practices. Therefore, many private customs continued. When death occurred at home, which was common in both towns and cities, the people (and even animals) were woken up. It was a neighbourly duty to function as a 'first responders', and neighbours would take the lead in the funerary process. The mirrors were covered, candles lightened and the windows opened.[6] These practices were meant to provide the soul of the deceased a free passage and to prevent spirits from wandering, all much discordant with Calvinistic views on death. These customs continued well into the early twentieth century.

2.2. THE EIGHTEENTH AND NINETEENTH CENTURIES

Having a 'decent' funeral became a matter of increasing concern from the seventeenth century onwards. 'Decent' meant that one was expected to pay for their own funeral costs, yet not every citizen could afford this. In the countryside and in small communities limited funds and facilities existed to conduct funerals. Moreover, certain provisions in the cities, such as the placing of the tombstone, had become outrageously expensive and were affordable only for the elite. To make funerals available to all, a variety of religious or neighbourly societies (evolved from the practice of neighbourly duty), associations, companies, undertakers and insurers emerged throughout the country.[7] Neighbourly societies took on this

---

[6]Kok (2005), p. 174.

[7]Cappers, W. (2012). *Aan deze zijde van de dood. Funeraire componenten van seculariserende cultuurlandschappen in Nederland 1575-2010.* Arnhem. Unpublished PhD thesis.

responsibility in the rural areas, and the guilds did so in the cities. The guilds collected funds, called the death debt or *doodscout*, to safeguard the funerals of their members. The death debt was either paid by the next of kin or by the deceased during life.[8]

When the guilds were disbanded in 1798, their funeral funds, referred to as *dodenbossen* or *dodenbussen*, had acquired such a significant place in society that they continued to exist as independent funeral societies. They expanded over time and became common organisations in Dutch society. It is estimated that in 1880 over 430 funeral societies existed, and that half of the Dutch had a membership with an average amount of insured capital of 60 Dutch Guilders, enough to pay for one's last rites.[9] The names of funeral societies, such as 'For Everyone's Wellbeing' and 'Help in Need after Death', continued to reflect the tradition of good neighbourly relations (Image 2.1).[10]

The eighteenth century is typically referred to as the Age of Reason. Although scholars have observed changing attitudes towards death during the Enlightenment, funerary practices in the Netherlands hardly altered. Elsewhere in Europe, burials inside and around churches were halted due to health and safety concerns. In the Netherlands, the incorporation of this new prohibition would be a slow process.

In 1784 the Holy Roman Emperor Joseph II, the Austrian emperor who still reigned over certain parts of the Southern Netherlands issued an edict that embargoed church burials. In France, Napoleon issued a decree which forbade burials in

[8]Kok (2005), pp. 213–214.
[9]Kok (2005), p. 214.
[10]Kok (2005), p. 214.

Image 2.1. Code of the Funeral Association *Tot Aller Welzijn* ('For Everyone's Wellbeing').

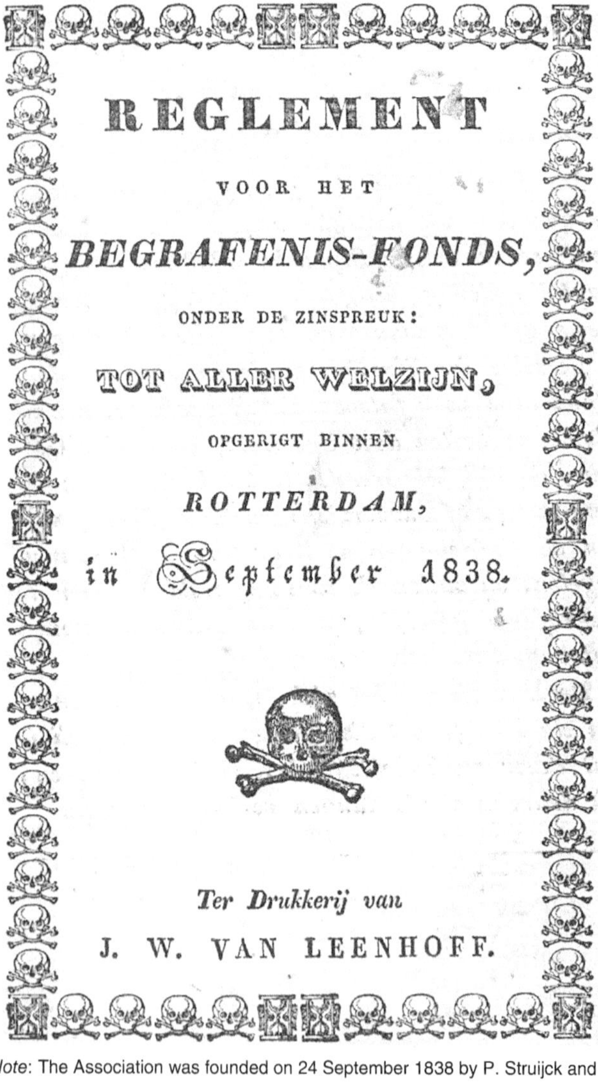

REGLEMENT

VOOR HET

BEGRAFENIS-FONDS,

ONDER DE ZINSPREUK:

TOT ALLER WELZIJN,

OPGERIGT BINNEN

ROTTERDAM,

in September 1838.

Ter Drukkerij van

J. W. VAN LEENHOFF.

Note: The Association was founded on 24 September 1838 by P. Struijck and T. Wylacker in Rotterdam, Zuid-Holland.

Source: Historical Collection National Nederlanden.

churches and ordered cemeteries to be placed outside of urban areas. The Netherlands has been a vassal state since 1795, and only in 1810, when the country effectively fell under the Napoleonic Empire, the *Code Pénal* was applied. However, the custom of burying in churches was hard to break, and the establishment of cemeteries on the outskirts of town did not really develop. Other French innovations like the introduction of the first Constitution, the Civil Code, civil registry, conscription, cadastre, surnames, house numbers and standard (metric) sizes and weights were adopted less reluctantly. The new civil registry made death registration compulsory and uniform: the attendance of a witness was required at registration, and the cause of death would from now on be registered.

When the Netherlands became an independent Kingdom again in 1813, King Willem I kept all the aforementioned modernisations but overturned the Napoleonic burial laws. However, in 1827 the same king issued a royal decree which ordered towns with over a thousand inhabitants to establish cemeteries on the outskirts. Due to a rapid growth of the population and increasing health issues, which resulted in an immense pressure on burial space, burial conditions had become deplorable. The decree found some response, although the newly established burial spaces were often too small and not far enough out of town. They filled up quickly and rapidly became enclosed by urban areas again.

It would take up till 1869 for these measures to be laid down in a first Burial Law. This legislation not only banned burials in churches, but also placed municipalities in charge. Each municipality had to provide a 'general' cemetery for its inhabitants, and therefore churches were no longer the sole providers of burial space. The new situation encouraged notions of a 'decent burial place', a worthy and dignified place for the dead. In concordance with emerging Romantic notions of death, graves were envisioned in romantic landscaped burial parks and a golden age for landscape architects flourished.[11]

Although the shift from burials in churches to burials in (general) cemeteries led to an increase of funerary options, nineteenth-century Roman Catholic or Protestant church services remained important and rather uniform. Most funerals highly depended on the involvement of neighbours and the local community, and regional and local traditions prospered. In some Protestant communities, the funeral did not take place in church at all. Instead, the deceased was buried at the local cemetery by the next of kin and the local community. If a minister was present, a prayer would be said at the grave. In some regions, especially in the provinces of Friesland and Overijssel, the tradition to walk with the deceased around the cemetery (*omgang*) prior to burial continued throughout the century.[12] Moreover, a wide variety of mourning garments were common in the country. Special attire, cloaks and jewellery, as well as richly decorated wooden funerary hatchments (*rouwborden*), special lanterns and bells were used to indicate the occurrence of death at a home.

By the late nineteenth century cemeteries were increasingly managed in a practical and business-like fashion. This resulted in organised and uniform graves, although both Protestants and Catholics had their own sections at cemeteries and developed their own unique grave-decorating styles. Protestants expressed a preference for attributes that symbolised the finiteness of life: open bibles, extinguished torches, cracked pitchers, empty hourglasses, urns, laurel wreaths and pillars as well as a great number of suitable Bible quotations.

---

[11]Spruit, R. (1986). *De dood onder ogen*. Houten: De Haan, 80–85; Raak, C. (1995). *Dodenakkers*. Amsterdam: Arbeiderspers, 18.
[12]Kok (2005), p. 314.

Catholics emphasised the bond between the living and the dead, symbolised by the omnipresent Christ on the cross and interceding angels and saints. The prayer chapels at or near cemeteries reflect the Catholic requirement that believers should be buried in proximity of a church (see Section 7.2.1).

2.3. THE EARLY TWENTIETH CENTURY

In 1914 the First World War began. Whereas the Netherlands remained neutral, its neighbouring countries suffered an immense death toll. The Dutch only experienced the devastation and cruelties of the war from the side lines, and although the Dutch Army was mobilised throughout the conflict they were mainly concerned with the housing of refugees, the guarding of internment camps for captured soldiers, and the prevention of smuggling. Historic debates on the impact of the War on attitudes towards mortality are limited in the Netherlands, and the Dutch did not at that time develop a practice of a national commemorative culture in which the military played a leading role. This would slightly change after the Second World War, the first war the Dutch would be involved in for over a century.

In 1914 another event occurred in the Netherlands that would significantly impact future funerary practice – more so than the First World War. On April 1 the first cremation took place, even though it was not mentioned as an option for disposal in the 1869 Burial Law. The authorities prosecuted those responsible for allowing and assisting in this cremation, but the Supreme Court eventually ruled the cremation not a criminal offence.[13] The Association to

[13]Cappers, W. (1999). *Vuurproef voor een grondrecht. Koninklijke vereniging voor facultatieve crematie 1874-1999*. Zutphen: Walburg Pers, 127–148.

Image 2.2. Image of the Westerveld Crematorium in Driehuis-Velsen in 1913, the Year of Its Opening.

Note: The first cremation, of Dr C.J. Vaillant, took place on 1 April 1914.
Source: Archief Crematorium Westerveld, Driehuis.

Introduce Cremation in the Netherlands – *De Vereeniging tot Invoering der Lijkverbranding in Nederland* – founded in 1874, had lobbied tirelessly for legislation. They campaigned to bring cremation to the attention of the Dutch and to make it a practical and legal option. They even had – provisionally – built their own crematorium which opened in 1913 (Image 2.2). The cremationists in the Netherlands, as they did elsewhere in Europe, pictured cemeteries as breeding grounds for germs and epidemics to which cremation would offer a hygienic solution. In addition, they argued that cremation would result in lower cemetery maintenance and would decrease pressure on land, especially in the cities.[14] In 1919

[14]Adams, A. & Schrauwen, A. (1992). *Ontwerpthema: Crematie*. Delft: Publikatieburo TU Delft, 42.

the Workers' Association for Cremation – *de Arbeiders Vereeniging Voor Lijkverbranding* (AVVL) – added its emancipatory ideals to the cremation agenda: cremation was propagated as the great equaliser. While the cremation movement gained foothold early on, and cremations were not legally sanctioned, it would only be legislated in 1955.

In the following decade, some Protestant churches and the Catholic Church formally accepted cremation as a legitimate form of bodily disposal, although they would remain favourable towards burial. In accordance with the depillarisation and the diminishing influence of the churches, cremation numbers rose explosively from the 1970s onwards. In 1991, burial and cremation became equal in terms of law and since 2003 cremation has been the most popular form of bodily disposal in the Netherlands.

2.4. THE LATE TWENTIETH CENTURY

After the Second World War, the government expanded the welfare system. Dutch citizens increasingly gained access to health care and schooling, and more people shared in the economic prosperity. The gaps between social classes evaporated to a great extent and life expectancy rose considerably. Confidence grew in civil decency and the socially engineered society, and (religious) concerns about death and dying moved to the background.[15] As the structural avoidance and sequestration of death advanced in society, death and remembrance practices were further sobered down. Funerals were simplified, the grave coverings at cemeteries were practical and modest,

[15]Cappers (1999), pp. 127–148.

and no public markers of grief were expressed. Crematoria emerged at the outskirts of towns and near highways. Furthermore, traditional mourning clothing practically disappeared, making grief invisible. Also, the phenomenon of a national day of mourning, marking the death of renowned individuals or victims of accidents and disasters, became highly exceptional.[16] The only official and public commemoration – annually since 1947 – is the National Remembrance of the Dead (*Dodenherdenking*) on the 4th of May at 8 p.m. During a national ceremony on Dam Square in Amsterdam and at local war monuments, 'all Dutch war victims – civilians and soldiers' – are remembered, 'who died or were killed in the Kingdom of the Netherlands or anywhere in the world since the outbreak of the Second World War, as well as in later war situations and during peace operations' (see also Section 9.2.1).[17]

From the late 1980s onwards, death practices became public and dynamic. Society had become increasingly unchurched, individualised and multicultural. Funerals were becoming tailor-made, and in addition to professionals the next of kin began to play an active role in the funerary process. A thorough revision of the Corpse Disposal Act in the 1990s would accommodate the funerary needs of Dutch citizens with increasingly diverse backgrounds.[18] It became possible, for example, to conduct shroud burials and a wide range of ash

---

[16]The only occasions for this in the Netherlands were the death of Queen Wilhelmina in 1962, the death of US President Kennedy in 1963 and the MH17 disaster in 2014.

[17]Retrieved from https://www.4en5mei.nl/herdenken-en-vieren/veelgestelde-vragen/achtergrondinformatie-herdenken/wie-herdenken-we/wat-is-het-memorandum. Accessed on March 16, 2019.

[18]Whereas the revisions of the Act accommodated new practices, it is important to note that accommodating many different practices is an integrated part of Dutch society and policy. Due to the countries' pillarised history, diversity has been firmly rooted in the legal system.

disposal practices. Moreover, questions concerning the end-of-life entered the public debate, and in 2001 euthanasia became a legal practice in the Netherlands. While the debates on euthanasia long focused on medical and ethical aspects, questions of a 'good death' and 'good dying process' have now been brought to the table. The medicalisation and institutionalisation of death and dying have become subject of debate.

From the 1990s, there have been several other noteworthy developments in the Dutch funerary landscape, and these will be discussed through the various sections in the book.

CHAPTER 3

DEMOGRAPHIC AND LEGAL FRAMEWORKS

3.1. MORTALITY IN THE NETHERLANDS

Between 1950 and 2018 the Dutch population increased from 10 to 17 million people. Life expectancy was boosted by 10 years to an average of 81.5.[1] As a result of the ageing and growing population, the yearly number of deaths more than doubled from 75,900 in 1950 to 153,328 in 2018. In 1966 the absolute number of deaths for the first time exceeded 100,000. The mortality rate dropped between 2002 and 2011 due to the absence of severe flu waves and extreme weather conditions.[2] However, the number of deaths has

[1]CBS (2019). Retrieved from https://opendata.cbs.nl/statline/#/cbs/nl/dataset/37360ned/table?dl=10917. Accessed on March 11, 2019. The governmental institution that gathers and presents statistical information about the Netherlands is called Statistics Netherlands or CBS – Centraal Bureau voor de Statistiek. They provide regular, longitudinal and quantitative data that can be easily accessed or requested online via https://opendata.cbs.nl

[2]UitvaartBranchemonitor (2018). *Stand van de uitvaartbranche 2017*. Den Haag: Uitvaartmedia.

since been on the rise. According to the current prognosis it will increase to 204,787 deaths per year in 2050.[3]

3.1.1. Place of Death

In 2016 one-third of deaths in the Netherlands occurred at home (32.8%). The majority of deaths took place in institutional settings: a hospital (24%), a nursing home (26.2%) or an elderly home (8%); 9% of deaths occurred elsewhere.[4]

3.1.2. Causes of Death

In 2017 dementia, lung cancer, stroke, coronary heart disease and heart failure were the top five causes of death, leading to the highest mortality. From the perspective of disease groups, most people died of cancer and benign tumours (31%) and of cardiovascular diseases (25%).[5]

3.2. LEGAL FRAMEWORKS

The Dutch House of Representatives (*Tweede Kamer*) cooperates with The Senate (*Eerste Kamer*) to create formal legislation. Laws reflect societal debates, and the process of creating legislation is also influenced by industry. Debates on death care, funerary provisions, and methods of bodily disposal, as well as related topics like organ donation and

---

[3]Retrieved from https://opendata.cbs.nl/statline/#/CBS/nl/dataset/83794NED/table?dl=1D1D2. Accessed on April 10, 2019.
[4]CBS (2016). *Sterfte naar plaats van overlijden.* Maattabel nr. 170183.
[5]https://www.volksgezondheidenzorg.info/ranglijst/ranglijst-doodsoorzaken-op-basis-van-sterfte. Accessed on March 11, 2019.

euthanasia, are regularly put on the agenda of parliamentary debates.[6]

3.2.1. The Euthanasia Act

Euthanasia – the termination of life by a doctor at the voluntary and well-considered request of a patient, in very specific cases and under very specific circumstances – was legalised in the Netherlands in 2001.[7] The 'Act on the termination of life on request and assisted suicide' – in everyday parlance referred to as *the Euthanasia Act* – came about after three decades of public debate, during which numerous consultations took place with medical, ethical, legal, political and religious experts as well as with patients and their family members.[8]

Euthanasia and physician-assisted suicide are not punishable in the Netherlands when the attending physician acts in accordance with two criteria of 'due care'. First, only the physician can terminate the patient's life. Second, the physician must administer the euthanatics properly. In the case of assisted suicide, the physician must provide the euthanatic to the patient and must remain present until death occurs. In addition to the criteria of due care the physician must notify the municipal coroner of the cause of death. Also, she/he must report the euthanasia to a review committee. The

---

[6]For an overview of parliamentary debates, see https://www.tweedekamer.nl/kamerstukken

[7]For the full act, de *Wet toetsing levensbeëindiging op verzoek en hulp bij zelfdoding*, see https://wetten.overheid.nl/bwbr0012410/2018-08-01

[8]Van der Ven, J. (2013). 'On the brink of death. Euthanasia from the angle of law, morality and religion: a cross-cultural perspective'. In Venbrux, E. et al. (eds.). *Changing European death ways*. Munster: Lit Verlag, 25–70.

members of the committee assess the followed procedures. In 2017, 6,585 cases (4.4% of all deaths) of euthanasia and assisted suicide were reported to the authorities. In most instances the procedure was performed by the GP (85.6%).[9] Additionally, 17,900 people had made a euthanasia request for an imminent death and a further 67,700 people had made a euthanasia request for the distant future.

In order to facilitate euthanasia in the Netherlands, strict (medical) protocols had to be instated. For example, patients need to be lucid until the very end as they must provide verbal consent before the euthanatic is administered by the physician, who is the only one legally allowed to do so. The law assigns a mandatory role to physicians and has necessarily protocolled dying. Although only a small percentage of deaths results from euthanasia, its legalisation has had a significant impact on the ways in which dying in general is facilitated and formalised.

3.2.2. Corpse Disposal Act

The first national legislation on burial was passed in 1869. The so-called Burial Act replaced a rather incoherent patchwork of local regulations and royal decrees. The Act was significantly updated in 1955 in view of cremation, which was then legalised. The name of the Act changed to *Wet op de Lijkbezorging (Wlb)*, which can be literally translated as the Corpse Disposal Act.

In 1991 a completely renewed Wlb was implemented after it was first submitted to the House of Representatives in

[9]Regionale toetsingscommissies euthanasie (2017). *Jaarverslag*. Retrieved from Https://www.euthanasiecommissie.nl/de-toetsingscommissies/uitspraken/jaarverslagen/2017/mei/17/jaarverslag-2017. Accessed on March 11, 2019.

1971. In the memorandum of explanation, the government stated that the proposed draft aimed merely to update the existing funerary provisions. The excessive two-decade-long parliamentary treatment of this seemingly modest objective indicates the sensitivity of burial and cremation legislation. The 1991 Act has been constantly refined on minor issues, and jurisprudence has been impacting the interpretation and execution of the law.[10] In 1997 an additional legal order on the Corpse Disposal Act was issued, called the *Besluit op de lijkbezorging*. The additional order functions as a prescript to the practical execution of the Wlb.[11] It offers a clear and practical document for individuals, municipalities and the funerary industry to regulate common funeral practices in the Netherlands. Many aspects of the Wlb are enforced on a local level and is therefore laid down in municipal regulations.

A general overview of the Wlb reveals significant aspects of Dutch funerary practice and provides information for cross-cultural comparison. The Wlb contains eight chapters and 96 articles, of which the following sections provide a paraphrased summary.

3.2.2.1. Chapter I. General Provisions

The general provisions prescribe that the bodily disposal of a corpse (*lijkbezorging*) must take place through burial, cremation or other legally approved methods. The regulations apply to deceased adults, as well as to stillborn infants (born lifeless after a gestational age of at least 24 weeks).

[10]A complete overview of the legislation, updates and additional information is online accessible via https://wetten.overheid.nl/bwbr0005009/2018-08-01. Accessed on February 17, 2019.

[11]https://wetten.overheid.nl/bwbr0009080/2013-01-01. Accessed on February 17, 2019.

3.2.2.2. Chapter II. General Requirements for Bodily Disposal

Post-mortem and Identification. The deceased must be examined by a physician who, when she/he is convinced that the death has occurred naturally, provides a declaration of death. If not convinced, the municipal coroner will be summoned.

In the case of a termination of life on request or assisted suicide, the attending physician does not provide a declaration of death. Rather, the municipal coroner will be informed. In the notification, the physician includes a detailed report on compliance with the due care requirements as referred to in the Euthanasia Act.

A registration number must be affixed to the coffin (or to the other case holding the corpse), corresponding with the number on an attached document that includes the names of the deceased and the dates of birth and death, or the surname of the stillborn.

Leave for Burial or Cremation. Burial or cremation cannot take place without the written leave of the civil registry officer. Written permission is only granted when the death certificate has been issued by the attending physician or a municipal coroner, or when the prosecutor gives a statement of approval.

In addition to the death certificate, the physician registers the cause of death and related information for the purpose of national statistics.

Terms. Burial or cremation occurs no earlier than 36 hours after death, and no later than the sixth working day after death.

Provision in Funeral Services. The person who applies for the leave for burial or cremation at the civil registry is responsible for arranging the funeral services. The funeral services are provided according to the (presumed) wishes of the deceased, unless these cannot be reasonably accommodated. Deciding a final destination to the ashes of the deceased is considered a part of the funeral services.

Government Care. The Wlb assumes that the next of kin take care of the funeral. If there are no surviving relatives, the municipality arranges the funeral. The municipality must take into account the (presumed) wishes of the deceased, unless the realisation of the wishes of the deceased cannot reasonably be requested from the municipality.

3.2.2.3. Chapter III. Burial

General Provisions. Burial must take place at a municipal or 'special' (*bijzonder*) cemetery, and the cemetery has to be legally established. Graves are issued for a minimum of 10 years. The deceased must be buried either in a general or in a private grave. In the case of a general grave, the holder of the cemetery determines who is buried in it. In the case of a private grave, this is decided by the entitled person (the next of kin) with an exclusive right over the grave.

At least six months (general grave) or a year (private grave) before the rights on a grave expire, the cemetery manager shall notify the person concerned in writing. The rights on private graves can always be extended, provided the request is done two years before the rights end.

A corpse can only be exhumed with a permit from the mayor of the municipality where it is buried, and – in case of a private grave – with the permission of the person entitled to the grave. Necessary provisions regarding medical supervision, transport and destination of the corpse must be included in the permit. A permit is not needed when it concerns the final clearing of graves, provided this is done according to the cemetery regulations.

A permit/permission is not needed when the exhumation is ordered by a judicial authority for the purpose of a criminal investigation.

The Additional Legal Order on Bodily Disposal (*Besluit op de Lijkbezorging*, see Section 3.2.2.) further states that a corpse is to be buried in a coffin. Burial may take place without a coffin, provided that another covering is used that is appropriate for the purpose of burial. The coffin or covering should be made of biodegradable materials, with the exception of the handles, ornaments and the connecting elements such as glue, nails, screws, staples or clips.

Municipal Cemeteries. A municipality must have at least one municipal cemetery. In some cases, a number of municipalities may provide a cemetery together. Burials can take place every day at reasonable hours. The municipality may exclude Sundays and generally recognised public holidays, though the law does not prohibit burial on these days.

Special Cemeteries. A special cemetery has to be constructed and maintained by a denomination, a legal entity under private law or an individual. The commissioning of a special cemetery requires the permission of the mayor and the municipal executives. They may only refuse such permission if legal requirements are not met.

A denomination of any religion is entitled to have one or more denominational ('ecclesiastic') cemeteries. When the law refers to a cemetery, it indicates appropriate cemetery and burial space. The cemetery space for a denomination is proportional to the total amount of burial land in the municipality. Insofar as a denomination does not exploit a special cemetery, part of the municipal cemetery will be made available at request.

Closure and Removal of Cemeteries. If no burials have taken place for a period of 10 years, a cemetery can be formally closed by the mayor and the municipal executives. The cemetery should remain untouched for 20 years, and no new bodies can be interred.

3.2.2.4. Chapter IV. Cremation

General Provisions. Cremation must take place in a crematorium. The holder of the crematorium keeps a register of all the cremations and of the final destination of the ashes.

Crematoria. Both municipal and 'special' crematoria exist. A municipal crematorium is established and operated by the municipality, and must offer daily cremation opportunities at reasonable hours. The crematorium may be closed at Sundays and public holidays, though cremation at these days is not prohibited.

A special crematorium has to be established and operated by a denomination, a legal entity under private law or an individual. It is not required to follow legal opening hours, but planning permission from the mayor and the municipal executives is required to establish, expand or modify any crematorium.[12] Whereas cemeteries are part of local landscaping planning regulations, crematoria are often classified as industry. This specifically impacts the location at which crematoria can be built.

[12]Planning is legally regulated in the Spatial Planning Act (Wet ruimtelijke ordering). See https://www.infomil.nl/onderwerpen/ruimte/functies/func-crematoria/. Accessed on April 10, 2019.

Preservation, Destination and Storage of Ashes.

General

After cremation, the crematorium manager will preserve and store the ashes in one or more ash containers. The ash container is closed inscribed with the surname and initials of the deceased, as well as a registration number. On the request of the next of kin, (part of) the ashes can be stored in a different way or can be made available to them.

The crematorium safeguards the storage of the ash container for at least one month after the cremation. Subsequently, the crematorium manager ensures that the ash container is either (a) buried or placed in a designated place, (b) that the ashes are scattered, (c) that the ashes are made available to the next of kin who ordered the cremation or (d) that the ashes are sent abroad.

Placing of the Ash Container

An ash container can be buried or placed in a part of the crematorium that is specifically intended for this purpose. Alternatively, it can be buried in a grave, placed on top of a grave, or situated in a separate place in a cemetery. The ashes can also be stored at a repository elsewhere, away from the crematorium or cemetery grounds.

The final clearing of ash containers can be done by, or on behalf of, the crematorium or the burial place manager. However, it can only be removed with permission of the entitled party or after a period of 10 years. The removal is done by scattering the ashes.

Scattering of the Ashes

The manager of the crematorium or the burial place can scatter the ashes from an ash container at a site that is intended for permanent ash scattering or at open sea. S/he does so at the request of the next of kin or in view of the final clearing of the ash container.

3.2.2.5. Chapter V. Special Modes of Bodily Disposal

In the interest of science or academic education, and with written permission of the mayor, a corpse may be dissected. The Additional Legal Order on Bodily Disposal (*Besluit op de Lijkbezorging*, see Section 3.2.2) regulates the handling of the corpses of those who died or those who were stillborn on Dutch ships at sea. It regulates sea burials, as well as cases in which the corpse must be preserved.

3.2.2.6. Chapter VI. Special Provisions

A corpse may not be embalmed, nor may it be subjected to any other protective treatment that is not aimed at the use of parts of the corpse pursuant to the Organ Donation Act. This prohibition does not apply when the corpse is sent abroad or when it has been destined for dissection.

If the deceased has given permission, his corpse may be subjected to a section. When the deceased's consent is missing, permission for a section may be given by the spouse, the registered partner or another life companion. In the absence or inaccessibility of such a partner, the available adult relative may grant permission, or, if these are also unavailable, those who take care of the body. In the case of a criminal investigation these restrictions do not apply.

3.2.2.7. Chapter VII. Penal Provisions

This chapter lists several violations of the Wlb and their associated penalties. Depending on the severity of the violation, offenders may be charged with up to three months' detention or a third category fine, or with up to one-month detention or fine of the second category.

3.2.2.8. Chapter VIII. Transitional and Final Provisions

Transitional Provisions. The Wlb is continuously changing due to jurisprudence. This paragraph offers transitional regulations to manage the dynamics of the Act and its earlier legislative frameworks.

Final Provisions. The Act does not apply to the funeral services of members of the Royal family.

3.3. RECENT DEVELOPMENTS IN LEGISLATION

The Corpse Disposal Act is currently being modernised and under discussion at the House of Parliament. Following a note to create a new Funeral Act, published in November 2018, the minister of the Interior and Kingdom Relations has indicated that the government aims to make revisions.[13] The debate focuses on bodily disposal, well-being and on safeguarding the quality of the funeral industry. Proposed revisions include the legalisation of new forms of bodily disposal (see Section 3.3.1), and the removal of the one-month waiting period to retrieve the ashes from the crematorium. In the future, it is also likely that stillborn twins, as well as a mother and baby who have died in labour, can be buried or cremated together. Furthermore, the proposals mention the possibility that future burials or cremations can take place 20 hours after death, instead of 36 hours. The period within which the funeral must take place might be extended from six to eight working days. Round-table and parliamentary discussions

[13]D66 (2018). *Initiatiefnota Moderne Uitvaartwet.* The note can be accessed via https://d66.nl/content/uploads/sites/2/2018/11/Initiatiefnota-Moderne-Uitvaartwet.pdf; further information can be found in the Parliamentary papers (*Kamerstukken*) 2018–2019, 30696-44.

have been held in April and May 2019, and the process is ongoing.[14]

3.3.1. Resomation, Cryomation and Compostation

The Dutch funeral industry and the Dutch government are exploring new forms of bodily disposal. The most discussed methods are resomation, cryomation and compostation, of which the first is considered the most serious possibility for the near future. Resomation – also referred to as water cremation or alkaline hydrolysis – is the dissolution of the corpse in a mixture of water, potassium hydroxide and reaction liquid.[15] The hydrolysis process takes place under pressure in a purpose-built tank. It results only in bone that – once dried and cremulated – forms a white powder. The resomated remains can be disposed by the next of kin.[16] Further research is needed to make resomation a legal possibility. Safety analyses have already been performed and a survey has shown that the majority of the Dutch population does not object to legalising resomation.[17] In fact, about 25% of the Dutch would consider resomation a possible

[14]In view of the parliamentary discussions in May 2019, members of parliament have submitted motions concerning the note, which can be accessed via https://www.tweedekamer.nl/kamerstukken/stemmingsuitslagen/detail?id=2019P09241&fbclid=IwAR1OtvZmbvzGBAAmTdqlMsHm_eIBFa0FR2pRtVdxTpBhFbpxyihgShvQW6A; in view of the parliamentary round-table discussion in April 2019, a number of experts, branche organisations and funeral companies have submitted position papers concerning the note, which can be accessed via https://www.tweedekamer.nl/debat_en_vergadering/commissievergaderingen/details?id=2019A00642

[15]Alkaline hydrolysis is the technical term for resomation. In Dutch parlance the term resomation is used.

[16]TNO-Rapport (2018). *Veiligheidsanalyse resomeren.* TNO 2018 R10677.

[17]TNO-Rapport (2018); I&O Research (2017). *Rapport draagvlakonderzoek resomeren.* Rapportnummer 2017/028.

alternative.[18] The Technical University Delft has created an assessment framework for testing new forms of bodily disposal, which considers values such as sustainability, autonomy, religious freedom and bodily integrity.[19] The Health Council of the Netherlands has been asked to assess new forms of bodily disposal – especially resomation and compostation – on the basis of this framework.[20] Results are expected in 2020.

3.3.2. Changes in the Personal Records Database

On 18 December 2018, the Dutch senate approved an amendment of the Personal Records Database Act – *Basisregistratie Personen (BRP)* – to enable the registry of children who are no longer alive at the time of birth, or retroactively concerning children born lifeless in the past – for whom a certificate was drawn up stating the child is no longer alive, issued by Dutch authorities. The amendment was the result of a petition from parents whose stillborn child had not been eligible for registration in the BRP, and therefore seemed to have never existed. The parents regarded this as factually incorrect and a cause of major grief. From February 2019 onwards, parents can submit a request to include their lifeless child in the BRP.[21] The child's name and

---

[18] I&O Research (2017).

[19] TU Delft (2018). *Beoordelingskader alternatieve vormen van lijkbezorging*. Delft: Design for Values Institute, 9.

[20] The letter of minister Ollongren to the Health Council of the Netherlands (DGBRW 2018-0000931392) can be accessed via https://www.gezondheidsraad.nl/documenten/adviezen/werkprogramma/werkprogramma/01/toelaatbaarheid-nieuwe-vormen-van-lijkbezorging

[21] https://www.eerstekamer.nl/wetsvoorstel/34882_wijziging_van_de_wet. Accessed on March 12, 2019.

details will be listed and appear on an excerpt of the BRP and via mijnoverheid.nl. In this way their child and their parenthood is formally being recognised.

3.3.3. Recent Jurisprudence

The Corpse Disposal Act (Wlb) is further defined by case law, which means that current rulings are guided by earlier jurisprudence.

The following two examples give an indication of the legislative dynamics:[22]

- *Court of Limburg (ECLI:NL:RBLIM:2017:1272)* The deceased had appointed his wife as the executor of his will, and had left instructions for the funeral. His wife, however, has been placed under administration due to her health (dementia). One son wished to scatter the ashes in Maastricht, the other son preferred to bury them in Roermond. The subdistrict court judge was asked to make a judgement on the final destination of the ashes. First, the judge observed that article 18 of the Wlb takes precedence over the will. Thus the (presumed) wish of the deceased determines the manner of funeral, including the final destination of the ashes. However, the wife cannot clarify her husband's (presumed) wish due to her illness. Subsequently, in view of the common desire to give both children the opportunity to commemorate, the subdistrict court finds a compromise: scattering in Roermond. The judge furthermore determined that the ashes may not be scattered until six months after the death of the living

[22]https://www.stimulansz.nl/wetgeving-en-jurisprudentie-wet-op-de-lijkbezorging/

spouse, which is to be expected in the short term, so that both spouses can be scattered together.

- *Court of East Brabant (ECLI:NL:RBOBR:2018:4415)* In a DELA funeral wishes booklet (see Section 6.3.1), the deceased had indicated that she wanted her ashes to be scattered. One of the two daughters had ordered the funeral and intended to follow her mother's wish. The other daughter then legally seized the urn, because she wished to keep a 'teaspoon' of ashes in a piece of jewellery. She argued that the deceased had given permission for this. The subdistrict court judge disagreed since there was no evidence of permission in the DELA funeral booklet.

There are numerous laws and national as well as municipal regulations that apply to certain aspects of death, dying, funerals and the funerary industry. As these rather fragmented regulations require a clear context they will be referred to in the regarding chapters: legislation concerning environmental protection (e.g. emissions from crematoria – see Section 8.6.6), historic preservation (e.g. grave monuments and cemeteries – see Section 7.3.6), environmental planning (e.g. crematorium see Section 8.6.7, and cemeteries see Section 7.2), working conditions legislation and the collective labour agreement for the funeral industry (see Section 4.2.2) and financial supervision (e.g. funeral insurances see under Section 4.2.1).

CHAPTER 4

THE FUNERAL DIRECTING INDUSTRY

Over two-thirds of the Dutch are insured for the inevitable: their own funeral. The Netherlands has the highest coverage level of funeral insurance in the world, which accounts for the country's highly professionalised and customer-oriented funeral directing industry. This exceptionally high coverage also means that the influence of these insurance companies – and the services related to them – should not be underestimated. Through the insurance plan they engage in life-long relations with their customers and are directly involved in many aspects of funeral organisation. They therefore have a significant impact on (the development of) funerary practices in the Netherlands. This chapter introduces the professional funerary landscape. It traces some historic roots and explores its current organisation, players, places and public appearances.

4.1. HISTORIC DEVELOPMENT

The roots of the funeral directing industry can be found in the ancient local and often rural traditions of 'good neighbourship' or 'neighbourly help' – *goed nabuurschap* or *burenhulp* – and in the many medieval funeral societies that were associated to the guilds, associations of artisans or craftspeople (see Section 2.2).[1] The structure of today's funeral industry developed further in the late nineteenth and early twentieth centuries. By then, a large portion of daily life in the Netherlands was organised along religious and ideological lines. Four pillars – Catholic, Protestant, Socialist and Liberal groups – had acquired a dominant position in society by creating a solid masonry of their own media, political parties, schools, sport clubs and indeed funeral societies.

Emancipatory ideals thrived within the pillars and this reinforced the pursuit for equal funeral opportunities. The establishment of funeral societies reached a peak between the 1900s and 1920s, especially in the northern part of the country. By the end of the First World War local societies began to expand to a national scale. In this period the first cooperatives emerged and the three largest players of the contemporary funeral directing industry came into existence. Current day funeral organisations Yarden, Monuta and DELA, each find their roots in a specific pillar. The Workers Association for Cremation – *de Arbeiders Vereeniging voor Lijkverbranding* (AVVL) – was established in Amsterdam in 1919. They merged with the Dutch Funeral and Insurance Association – *de Nederlandse Uitvaart en Verzekerings Associatie* (NUVA) – to the funeral and insurance organisation Yarden in 2001. The Apeldoorn Funeral Society – *de Apeldoornsche Begrafenisvereeniging* – was founded in 1923, and

[1] Kok, H. (2005). *Thanatos. De geschiedenis van de laatste eer*. Heeswijk-Dinther: Berne Media.Venhorst, C. & Mathijssen, B. (2017). *Dood. Wegwijs in de Nederlandse uitvaartcultuur*. Almere: Parthenon.

developed into the Monuta Trust in 1955. The (Protestant) Christian heritage of the society is reflected in the name *mors Ianua vitae*: death is the gateway to life. In 1937, the improvement of local burial facilities was discussed in a pub in Eindhoven, in the southern and dominantly Roman Catholic area of the Netherlands. Following these discussions, the Cooperative Mutual Burial Association Bear Each Other's Burden – *de Coöperatieve Onderlinge Begrafenisvereniging Draagt Elkanders Lasten* – was set up in the same year, an organisation which is the basis of the contemporary funeral cooperation DELA.

4.2. CURRENT ORGANISATION

The funeral directing industry in the Netherlands is best described as a growing mosaic of private funeral companies, public funeral organisations and regional and national trade associations. The number of enterprises has rapidly increased from 1110 in 2007 to 2190 in early 2019.[2] In terms of revenue the industry has grown by almost 20%, from €1 bn in 2010 to €1.2 bn in 2016.[3] Most new funeral companies have been started by small entrepreneurs, and today only 8% of the companies has over five employees (Chart 4.1). The funeral directing industry is thus facing increasing diversification and fragmentation.

---

[2]CBS (2019). Retrieved from http://statline.cbs.nl/Statweb/publication/?VW=T&DM=SLNL&PA=81589NED&D1=0-10&D2=1467-1468&D3=2,l&HD=181203-1335&HDR=G2&STB=G1. Accessed on February 2, 2019.

[3]Retrieved from https://www.nrc.nl/nieuws/2017/09/07/vergrijzing-uitvaartbranche-groeit-door-stijging-sterfgevallen-12876631-a1572542. Accessed on December 3, 2018.

Chart 4.1. Number of Funeral Companies and Employees in 2007 and 2019.

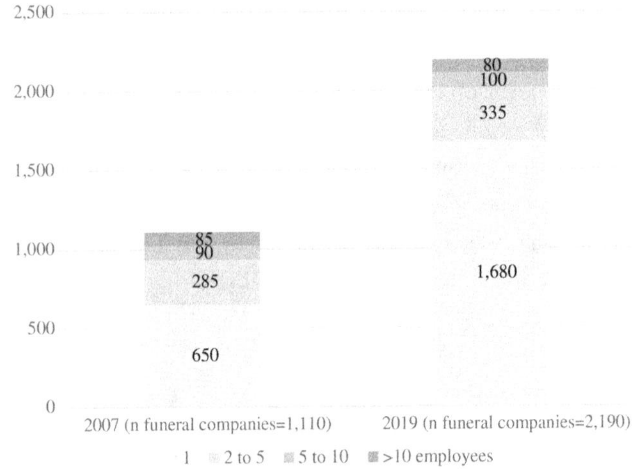

Source: CBS. (2019). Accessible via https://www.cbs.nl/nl-nl/nieuws/2017/36/de-uitvaartbranche-een-bescheiden-groeier

4.2.1. Types of Funeral Organisations

Today we can distinguish different types of funeral organisations. Funeral associations (*uitvaartverenigingen*) are non-profit organisations. By paying fees to the association, members are entitled to a (partially) paid funeral. The board is responsible for safeguarding and investing funds and securities to subsequently pay the funeral fees of members. As regulated by law there is an annual general meeting in which members can ask questions and vote on a variety of matters, such as possible changes in the insurance policy or the election of new board members. Certain decisions cannot be made without the members' vote, the details of which are specified in the statutes of the association. When a death occurs members can bring in the funeral director of their choice. Sometimes associations have the capacity to organise the funeral themselves. Although they may employ their own staff or use outsourcing, they typically work with volunteers, for instance to perform administrative duties. Most funeral associations emerged as local initiatives, finding their origins in the aforementioned tradition of neighbourly help and in the funeral funds of the guilds. Today an increasing number of them is struggling to find new (board) members, and many have been taken over by larger cooperatives or insurers.[4] Funeral foundations (*uitvaartstichtingen*) are similar to associations in terms of origins, aim and non-profit character. The most important difference is that they do not have members and thus no general meeting is held. This makes them less democratic, yet they can act more decisively.

Funeral cooperatives (*uitvaartcoöperaties*) consist of both an association and a business. They have the associations' democratic membership structure, but also aim to make a profit for their members to meet their specific material or financial needs. Usually different associations, organisations or branches merge into a larger cooperative to increase scale and reduce costs. By doing so, the cooperative aims to benefit its members. Cooperatives thus can provide funeral insurance (see below) as well as funeral directing services. Their business entity is typically organised as a *naamloze vennootschap* (NV) or *besloten vennootschap* (BV).[5] Cooperatives work at

[4]See, for example: https://www.rtvnoord.nl/nieuws/183292/Uitvaartverenigingen-luiden-de-noodklok. Accessed on December 3, 2018.

[5]These are the two most common business entities in the Netherlands, which are registered at the Netherlands Chamber of Commerce. Associations and foundations are also registered here.

a national or regional level, and they have local funeral homes. Thus, in various town or cities, funeral homes of the same cooperative may exist. Alternatively, there may be local franchises. These often are the result of a merger with private or family-run funeral directors.

Private funeral directors (*zelfstandige uitvaartondernemers*) are small-scale businesses that provide local or regional funeral care. They usually have a maximum of five employees, and many are family-owned and managed. Recently, specialised funeral directors have emerged to serve particular groups in Dutch society. Some focus on Creole Surinamese or Muslim funerals, for example, whereas others provide budget funerals, creative services or women-only funeral directors.

Funeral insurers (*uitvaartverzekeraars*) play a profound role in the Netherlands. Today 12 funeral insurance companies exist. Each of them is organised as an NV which means that they are owned by shareholders. De Nederlandsche Bank, the independent central bank in the Netherlands, monitors their financial position. The five largest insurers – Ardanta, DELA, Monuta, Yarden and Nuvema – provide funeral insurance policies to over 9 million Dutch citizens.[6] Of those above the age of 35, 70% pay a monthly fee and are insured for (part of) their funeral costs. Unlike associations, insurers are profit based and operate on a national scale. Some funeral insurers not only provide insurance policies, but also funeral care. Examples are DELA, Monuta and Yarden. They are constructed as holding companies under which various branches are classified. These branches can also include non-profit associations. The tasks of employees within these branches are usually limited to a specific

[6]Retrieved from https://www.uitvaartverzekering.nl/onderwerpen/welke-uitvaartverzekeraars-zijn-er. Accessed on December 3, 2018.

expertise, such as funeral services, funeral insurance, a funeral or deposit fund, an association or a franchise.

Franchisees (*franchisenemers*) work as self-employed entrepreneurs within the larger cooperatives or firms.

4.2.2. Trade Associations

Many Dutch funeral organisations, both private and municipal, are affiliated to trade associations. This includes funeral directing and insurance companies, but also crematoriums, mortuaries, thanatopraxy experts and suppliers of goods and hardware. The largest trade association is the Dutch Association of Certified Dutch Funeral Enterprises – *Brancheverenigíng Gecertificeerde Nederlandse Uitvaartondernemingen* (BGNU). With more than 200 affiliated funeral companies, they account for about 90% of the funerals in the Netherlands. The BGNU emerged in 2010 as a result of the merger between the Association for Entrepreneurs in the Funeral World – *Vereniging voor Ondernemers in de Uitvaartwereld* (VOU) – and the Dutch Association of Approved Funeral Entrepreneurs – *Nederlandse Vereniging van Erkende Uitvaartondernemers* (NUVU). The BGNU aims to influence legislation and policy regulations on a national level on behalf of the funeral sector. When funeral companies become a BGNU member, they benefit from the joint purchasing of goods and master agreements within the industry. The BGNU also owns the *Brancheblad Uitvaartzorg*, an independent journal for professionals that focuses on developments within the funerary profession.

In 2007 another important trade organisation was established, called NARDUS Cooperative Funeral Organisations – *NARDUS Samenwerkende Uitvaartorganisaties.* NARDUS emerged out of two earlier associations: the Dutch Association of Funeral Organisations – *Nederlands Verbond van Uitvaartorganisaties* (NVU) – and the Association of Non-Profit Funeral Societies – *Samenwerkingsverband van Uitvaartverenigingen zonder Winstoogmerk* (LSUW). NARDUS has a strong commitment to the traditional values of good neighbourly help. It represents the interests of local and regional funeral organisations and societies in particular.

NARDUS and the BGNU work together closely and supervise each other's plans and objectives for the funeral industry. NARDUS, for instance, has committed itself to creating opportunities for small entrepreneurs to obtain certificates, and tries to bridge the gap between small and large companies in the sector.

BGNU, NARDUS and the Employers' Association of Dutch Crematoria, together with national trade unions FNV, CNV and De Unie have negotiated a collective labour agreement (CAO) which applies to all private companies with activities within the funeral industry.[7] The *CAO Uitvaartbranche* prescribes terms of employment, wages and working hours, and is legally binding.[8] BGNU, NARDUS and the national trade unions have also agreed on a Health and Safety Catalog (*Arbocatalogus*) which has been tested positively by the Ministry of Social Affairs, and is used by the Labour Inspection as a frame of reference for enforcing health and safety legislation in the funeral industry.[9]

---

[7]Retrieved from https://business.gov.nl/regulation/cao/?fbclid=IwAR1-xMKCX75btdnp752ZVPNoarWT2zPZj3t6GXKKo0I-9JleRvT4mct5SD8. Accessed on April 14, 2019.

[8]Retrieved from https://www.uitvaart.nl/docs/CAO-Uitvaartbranche-2018-2020.pdf. Accessed on April 14, 2019.

[9]Retrieved from https://nardus.eu/wp-content/uploads/2013/05/Arbocatalogus-voor-de-uitvaartzorg-2010-02-19-34p-printvriendelijk.pdf. Accessed on April 14, 2019.

4.2.3. Education and Quality Management

Funeral directing in the Netherlands is an open profession. In theory any individual can start a funeral business without formal training or education.[10] In practice many funeral directors have had an education and participate in training programmes and courses. This is often supported by employers. It is also common for funeral directors to be trained on the job; skills, knowledge, and competencies are acquired whilst working in the field.

Currently various funeral directing courses exist in the Netherlands. They are provided by different organisations, such as Docendo, Meander Uitvaartopleidingen, Après la Vie Academie, GaandeweG Uitvaart Educatie, LOI and NHA. The courses vary in length – somewhere between 6 and 18 months – as well as in their approach. Some programmes consist of home study, whereas others are organised around group discussions and face-to-face meetings. Despite the variation in courses, all students take the same exam. The exam is created and provided by the Foundation for Funeral Care Examinations – *Stichting Vakexamens Uitvaartzorg* (Stivu). It tests seven main themes: Dutch language, general law, the Dutch Corpse Disposal Act, the day of the funeral, words to express mourning, finances for funeral care and contract forms. Students also write a report on their internship and take a face-to-face exam.

To safeguard the quality of the funeral directing industry and to protect customers the Foundation Quality Mark Funeral Care – *Stichting Keurmerk Uitvaartzorg* (SKU) – was established in 2006. The SKU introduced the Quality

[10]The same is true for starting a cemetery or crematorium – under the condition that the local authority provides (planning) permission.

Mark Funeral Care, which rapidly gained foothold in the Netherlands. To obtain the Quality Mark funeral companies submit to a comprehensive quality check and to an annual re-evaluation. Trade associations such as the BGNU and NARDUS work closely together with the SKU. A National Exam for Funeral Care – *Nationaal Vakexamen Uitvaartzorg* (NaVU) – was introduced in 2017 to further manage the quality of funeral directors. The exam focuses on both theory and practice. In the future all funeral directors will be obliged to pass this exam and associations such as the BGNU have made it one of the requirements to obtain the Quality Mark Funeral Care. For those with a lot of work experience but no formal training within the funeral directing industry, an alternative is offered to taking the exam.

4.2.4. Typical Premises of the Funeral Home

Most funeral homes are situated in the margins of cities and towns, near highway exits, hospitals, garden centres or industrial areas. Important exceptions are organisations that are located in listed buildings, hospices that are found in city centres, or small funeral shops or entrepreneurs in suburban areas. Usually though, the only funeral reference in a high-street or suburban shopping area is the local flower shop. Funeral homes can also be located at or near the cemetery or crematorium premises.

Funeral homes vary in terms of size and staffing. In a small funeral home, there usually are at least two people present. Larger funeral homes may employ 10 to 15 funeral directors. Depending on the time of day and the number of funerals, a variety of people will enter the premises: the manager or owner, funeral directors, mortuary technicians, volunteers, drivers, religious or civil celebrants, and the next of kin. The funeral homes of larger cooperatives and insurers typically follow a corporate identity in their design. They use the same colours, patterns and furniture throughout the country, and in some cases the funeral directors wear corporate clothes. Private funeral directors, on the other hand, design their funeral home on the basis of their own preferences and with the help of experts, such as architects, interior designers and fellow funeral directors.

While funeral homes differ in terms of their location, building, size and ownership, they typically share a range of provisions. There is a *welcoming hall*, through which people enter the building and where they are welcomed by staff. The next of kin may enter the funeral home for various reasons: to visit the deceased, to attend a wake, to participate in a memorial service, or for another type of appointment although discussion of the funeral arrangements takes place at people's homes. In addition to the welcoming hall, there typically is a *client office* with a large table. In this office, urns and remembrance objects may be on display and folders may provide information about funeral, cremation and burial practices and costs. Furthermore, an *employee office* can be found on the premises, as well as a *kitchen* with equipment – for employees and sometimes also for customers – and a *bathroom*. The funeral home also contains multiple *storage rooms*. These are used for coffins and other equipment. Flowers might have a separate storage room that is easily accessible to the florist as well as to the professionals that load the hearse. There is a garage or special parking place for the hearse, as well as *parking facilities* for clients and employees. Also, there will be a bicycle parking. Sometimes the funeral home has an auditorium for services (see Image 4.1), and there might be other amenities, such as a garden.

The funeral home functions as the temporary resting place for the deceased. Therefore, it has a *cooled room* and/or *freezer facility*, and there may also be a *morgue*. Moreover, the funeral

Image 4.1. A Small Auditorium in a Funeral Home in Overasselt, Gelderland.

Source: Photograph by Claudia Venhorst.

home is likely to have one or several *mourning rooms*, where the deceased can be laid to rest to be visited by the next of kin. The mourning room can be entered from within the funeral home, but often has a separate entrance too. Using a private key, the next of kin can visit their deceased 24/7 in the period before the funeral. The mourning room, or part of it, is usually cooled. Attached to it, one finds a private or common room where people can find coffee and tea in a small kitchenette.

4.3. CONTEMPORARY DEVELOPMENTS: GENDER, DIVERSITY AND HERITAGE

4.3.1. The Female Face of Death

Women have always played a role in death rituals. They assisted in taking care of the deceased or supported the next of kin. However, professional funeral care was long the exclusive domain of men. This has changed rapidly in the last three decades. Women have begun working as entrepreneurs, funeral directors, mortuary technicians, crematorium administrators and cremator experts. The emergence of female funeral professionals can be linked to the rise of personal funerals from the 1980s onwards. The disappearance of ecclesial rituals, which were often reserved for male professionals, has created room for women to create and perform funerals. In some new roles, like that of the civil celebrant, women form the majority.

The rise of female funeral experts has changed the face of the industry and has impacted people's expectations of funeral professionals. 'Female qualities' – such as warmth, empathy, care and an eye for detail – are frequently praised and deliberately used as marketing strategy, especially when it concerns representative roles and the personal contact with next of kin. Also, the popularity of women is often ascribed symbolic meaning associated with birth and rebirth. It thus might be no surprise that in 2006, one of the largest Dutch newspapers – *Trouw* – described the roles of funeral director and coffin bearer as 'ideal professions for women'.[11] The work of the funeral director also requires other, often contradictory, qualities. One has to be both empathetic and business-like, independent and a team player, organised and creative. The image of care that is associated with today's funerary profession often stands at odds with the highly regulated and organised reality. It is difficult to reconcile a commercial, business-like attitude

---

[11]Retrieved from https://www.trouw.nl/home/kistdrager-en-uitvaartverzorger-zijn-ideale-vrouwenberoepen-~ae474893/. Accessed on March 5, 2019.

with an excess of empathy and care. The role of gender within the funeral industry remains largely unexplored.

4.3.2. A Multicultural Funeral Home

As society becomes more diverse, so do its funerals. The increased number of Dutch people with diverse religious and cultural backgrounds has impacted the funeral directing industry. A large number of individual entrepreneurs have emerged in the funerary landscape, targeting 'newcomers' such as Muslims, spiritual seekers and those without religious affiliation. The funeral industry profession is increasingly accommodating multicultural funeral needs. In recent years, funeral directors, funeral associations and death studies scholars have collaborated through long-term courses and workshops to increase knowledge of diverse funeral wishes and to improve practical skills. This is an ongoing process of trial and error, and of learning, doing and collaborating.

In 2013, plans emerged to build a multicultural funeral home in Amsterdam to serve the city's future population. The aim was to provide practical, social and religious funeral facilities for various communities. To ensure that the multicultural home has a stable social foundation and is actually used by diverse groups, intrinsic intercultural solidarity is important. Yarden – the funeral company behind the initiative – therefore has brought people together from different religious and cultural groups to increase their familiarity with each other as well as the place.[12] Whereas the process

[12]Van der Pijl, Y. (2017). The birth of a multicultural funeral home. *Death Studies*. 41(1), 42–50.

has not been without challenges, the multicultural funeral home is expected to open its doors in 2019.

4.3.3. Reallocating Religious Heritage

Many churches and monasteries in the Netherlands are closing their doors due to a decrease in formal religious observance. Their buildings are often of great cultural and architectural value, and therefore many acquire a new purpose. They are being transformed into elderly homes, apartments, libraries or event halls. The Dutch funeral sector plays a role in maintaining and reallocating religious and cultural heritage.

In Eindhoven, for instance, the Mariënhage convent has been taken over by funeral company DELA. It aims to refurbish the church, monastery and former school to create a place that enables people to mark important moments in life, such as weddings and funerals.

Another example of repurposing can be found in the St. John the Baptist church in Arnhem, which was transformed into a funeral home and columbarium in 2013. The church provided space for funeral services, and mourning rooms that could be used by the next of kin to visit the deceased before the funeral took place. In addition to the columbarium, it hosted an urn crypt as well as possibilities for memorial plaques. Whereas the church building did receive some proper refurbishments, its doors were closed again in 2017. Due to lack of interest and income, the church building had to be sold. It now awaits a new use as a care or nursing facility with apartments.[13]

---

[13]Retrieved from https://www.gelderlander.nl/arnhem/wonen-en-zorg-functie-in-klarendalse-sint-jan-de-doperkerk~a2cb5706/. Accessed on April 11, 2019.

4.4. PUBLIC APPEARANCES: TELEVISED FUNERAL COMMERCIALS

The funeral directing industry in the Netherlands has a consumer-oriented character. This becomes most evident in the advertising campaigns and televised funeral commercials of funeral insurers and cooperatives that aim to grow their membership and to increase their viability. Although funeral advertising is not appreciated by everyone, and is sometimes considered inappropriate, the campaigns are common and highly visible within the public domain. On the one hand, they reflect funeral companies' understanding of Dutch death mentalities. On the other, they set people's expectations and perceptions of death and the funerary industry. Moreover, by discussing the event of death, advertising campaigns evidence and challenge aspects of the death taboo in society.

In 2011 the funeral organisation Monuta launched a campaign with the slogan 'It already is difficult enough for the immediate bereaved'.[14] A series of commercials was broadcast on national television, consisting of different episodes. In each episode, one witnesses the emotional-affective and practical struggles of the dearest and nearest bereaved. For example, we see a husband who has to choose a dress for his deceased wife, a daughter who has to travel back from abroad to attend the funeral and father who tries to access the Facebook account of his deceased daughter. The message? Losing someone is difficult, but we – the funeral professionals – can help. Importantly, the Monuta campaign draws attention to topics that often remain unspoken in the public domain, such as the grief of young adults or the loss of

[14]One of the commercials can be found via https://youtu.be/vkeYRCtzvKU, accessed on April 11, 2019.

a child. Also, it viscerally shows the emotions of ourselves and our loved ones. By doing so, the campaign encouraged people to think and speak about death.

In 2012 the funeral organisation DELA launched the campaign 'Why Wait Until It's Too Late?'.[15] In the televised commercial we do not see actors, but ordinary people who give a speech to express their love and gratitude to their significant others. In different episodes a football coach, a teacher and parents are put in the limelight. The people in the commercials also reflect the increasing cultural and religious diversity in the Netherlands. Except for the brand of the organisation itself, no trace of a funeral can be discovered in the commercial. Via the campaign DELA aims to emphasise that it is not only about a dignified farewell. Following the spirit of neighbourly help, it is about caring for each other. What you do to help other people in the here and now is what you will leave behind. Like Monuta, the DELA campaign invites the spectator to reflect on death during life. Moreover, it inspires the viewer to act accordingly.

In 2015, also funeral organisation Yarden launched a new and controversial campaign, with the slogan 'A good farewell takes you further'.[16] In the televised commercial we see theatre maker and actress Adelheid Roosen with an urn in her hands. She is reciting a poem about the funeral of her mother who passed away facing Alzheimer's disease. In the background a multicultural funeral spectacle is manifesting itself, and the commercial zooms in on various rites and practices. The commercial ends with Adelheid who reminds the viewer: 'We will die. Each and every one of us'. The first broadcasts

[15]One of the commercials can be found via https://youtu.be/N39-dCxM5aY, accessed on April 11, 2019.
[16]One of the commercials can be found via https://youtu.be/pBB8vUQckrE, accessed on April 11, 2019.

sparked laudatory but also angry reactions. Some people even requested to ban the advertisement. The controversy that emerged in the wake of the campaign shows that people have different understandings about what is appropriate and not. Above all, it evidences that death is a confrontation. The controversy itself indicates the social value of the Yarden campaign, and death campaigns in general.

CHAPTER 5

PAYING FOR FUNERALS

5.1. AVERAGE FUNERAL COSTS

In the Netherlands the average funeral costs between €6,500 and €11,000.[1] The average gross salary is €36,000, resulting in a monthly net wage of €2,120.[2] A 2017 study conducted by the National Institute for Budget Information (Nibud) shows that one in three people find it difficult to estimate their own funeral costs.[3] Funeral organisations usually give an overview of their funeral costs online. Also, they

---

[1]Different averages are given by different funeral providers, with a mean of €8,000. The specific amount strongly depends on personal preferences and local costs for the (urn) grave, the tombstone and the grave maintenance.

[2]Bureau for Economic Policy Analysis (2019). Retrieved from https://www.cpb.nl/sites/default/files/omnidownload/CPB-Kerngegevenstabel-raming-maart-2019_0.pdf; please note that Dutch citizens are obliged to pay monthly healthcare insurance, which minimally costs about €120 a month in 2019. Further healthcare insurance information is retrieved from https://www.nibud.nl/consumenten/zorgverzekering/. Accessed on May 11, 2019.

[3]Warnaar, M., Stoof, R. & Schonewille, G. (2017). *Kennis en bewustzijn van uitvaartkosten*. Utrecht: Nibud. The report is retrieved from https://www.nibud.nl/wp-content/uploads/Nibud-rapport-Kennis-en-bewustzijn-van-uitvaartkosten.pdf

encourage people to write down their funeral wishes, to keep them up to date and to set up a funeral insurance policy that would accommodate them. In addition, independent organisations exist that provide information and offer online tools to calculate one's funeral costs. The most important examples are the Nibud and the Consumers Association – *de Consumentenbond*. Lastly, a multitude of websites exists that compare services and offer advice. Examples are the funeral insurance guide – *de uitvaartverzekerinsgwijzer* – and the funeral calculator – *de uitvaartvergelijker*.

5.2. BREAKDOWN OF GENERAL, BURIAL AND CREMATION COSTS

The Nibud creates guidelines for funeral costs for local authorities and funeral professionals. These guidelines are used to establish prices for grave tenancy or cremation. They are also consulted when the local authority is paying for the funeral, for instance when the deceased has no next of kin. The funeral cost guideline is interesting because it is based on national averages. It thus provides a general breakdown of funeral, cremation and burial costs in the Netherlands. Table 5.1 gives an overview of the general costs, Table 5.2 of the burial costs and Table 5.3 of cremation costs.

Whereas the breakdown of expenses above gives an indication of funeral costs in the Netherlands, regional variation exists. Burial space may be increasingly scarce and more expensive in particular cities, and crematoria may calculate different prices. Moreover, more special or elaborate services impact the funeral costs: for example, a more expensive coffin, handmade mourning cards or more elaborate post-mortem care. Also the bereaved may hire additional celebrants or musicians, or go out to a pub or restaurant afterwards.

Table 5.1. Average Funeral Costs.

Type of Costs	Amount
Death certificate	€ 13
General tariff funeral director	€ 1,750
Mourning advert: announcement of death in regional newspaper	€ 500
Mourning postcards: announcement of death to be send to kith and kin (50 cards, excluding stamps)	€ 125
Transporting the deceased to the home or funeral home	€ 250
Post-mortem care (washing, dressing)	€ 150
Coffin (oak veneered chipboard)	€ 425
Lying the deceased in state at the funeral home, including visit to pay last respects	€ 475
Lying the deceased in state at home, including daily check up on the body and functioning of the cooling equipment	€ 475
Hearse	€ 250
Specialist vehicle following the hearse (usually for next of kin)	€ 250
Coffee table after the funeral (50 persons)	€ 250

Source: Warnaar et al. (2017, pp. 34–35).

In some cases, an extra expense may be calculated for Saturday funerals, even though Saturday is a regular day to conduct funerals in the Netherlands.

5.3. TYPES OF FUNERAL INSURANCE

Seventy per cent of Dutch citizens above the age of 35 have funeral insurance and pay a monthly fee to cover (part) of

Table 5.2. Average Burial Costs.

Type of Costs	Amount
Own grave (lease for 20 years for two persons), including maintenance and opening and backfilling of the grave	€ 3,500
General grave (lease for 10 years, grave is shared with strangers), including opening and backfilling on grave, Mondays–Fridays	€ 1,350
Burial in already existing grave (e.g. spouses)	€ 875
Simple gravestone	€ 1,000
Average gravestone	€ 2,500
Use of auditorium at cemetery (45 mins)	€ 220
Use of condolence room at cemetery	€ 175

Source: Warnaar et al. (2017, pp. 34–35).

Table 5.3. Average Cremation Costs.

Type of Costs	Amount
Crematorium (cremation, service in aula, use of condolence room)	€ 1,250
Technical cremation (only cremator, no ceremonial facilities)	€ 500
Ash dispersal at crematorium	€ 95
Safeguarding the ashes in crematorium bay (costs for one year)	€ 90

Source: Warnaar et al. (2017, pp. 34–35).

their future funeral costs.[4] Currently, 12 insurance companies exist at a national level.[5] They provide insurance policies or offer a combination of funeral insurance and funeral care. Endowment, in-kind or combined policies are the most popular types of funeral insurance today. The monthly fee is based on the starting age of the insured person, and on the amount of insured capital. For instance, the monthly fee for an endowment policy with a €5,000 lump sum, starting at the age of 40, costs about €8, which amounts to 0.4 per cent of the average net income.[6] Funeral insurance typically covers the cost of the services as depicted in Table 5.1, as well as the use of the auditorium and the actual technical cremation or burial. What is specifically included depends on the type and details of the particular policy. Funeral insurance does not cover the costs for the grave, tombstone or ash dispersal.

In the case of an endowment funeral policy (*kapitaal uitvaartverzekering*), the next of kin are paid a lump sum that must be spent on the funeral. The specific amount depends on the particulars of the insurance policy, and the next of kin can spend the lump sum at a funeral director of their own choosing. However, if the insurer also runs a funeral directing company, they will receive a larger sum if they choose that funeral director. This is framed as an extra benefit. Another option is in-kind funeral insurance (*natura uitvaartverzekering*), where the insurer has contracts with specific funeral directors. With an in-kind policy the next of kin receive services from a particular funeral director instead if a lump sum.

[4]Henselmans, M. (2017). *Laat je niet kisten door de commercie.* Oss: Genoeg.
[5]https://www.uitvaartverzekering.nl/onderwerpen/welke-uitvaartverzekeraars-zijn-er. Accessed on February 3, 2018.
[6]Nibud (2018). Retrieved from https://www.nibud.nl/consumenten/uitvaartverzekering/

Services include a funeral director, a hearse, a coffin and the auditorium space. It excludes the costs for the grave or the urn. For those who want a more elaborate funeral, the monthly insurance fee goes up or an extra sum is added to the funeral bill. Funeral insurers that offer in-kind policies often run their own funeral directing company. Therefore, and because of contracts with service providers, they make it unattractive for customers to switch funeral directors. Whereas an in-kind policy can be transferred into a lump sum, the amount you will receive is likely not enough to buy the same services elsewhere.

A third option is a combined funeral policy (*combinatie uitvaartverzekering*), incorporating aspects of the endowment and in-kind policy. This option is sometimes recommended because in-kind insurance might not cover the complete funeral costs. Twenty per cent of people with funeral insurance in the Netherlands are covered for less than €5,000, and 29% do not know the amount of insured capital.[7] By taking a combined policy, the lump sum can be used to pay for additional costs or more elaborate funeral wishes.

5.4. FUNERAL POVERTY AND MUNICIPAL HELP

Article 21 of the Corpse Disposal Act states that 'If no one provides the post-mortem care and funeral services in accordance with the law, the mayor takes care of this'. Local authorities in the Netherlands are legally obliged to pay for the funerals of those dying within their jurisdiction without next of kin, or to offer support when the next of kin have insufficient funds.

[7] Warnaar et al. (2017), p. 6.

Between 2010 and 2015, the number of municipally paid burials and cremations – *begrafenis of crematie van gemeentewege* – increased by 15%.[8] In 2016, 1 in 70 funerals was paid for by the local authority.[9] The reasons for this increase are currently unknown, and there are marked differences between municipalities. Some suggest the increase of municipal funerals results from of a decrease of funeral insurance and from higher debts, especially in the lower socio-economic classes.[10] When the local authority pays for the funeral, it becomes the client and hires a funeral director to arrange the funeral. As a client, the local authority makes the decisions. They will try to accommodate the deceased's wishes, especially regarding the type of bodily disposal. The burial or (technical) cremation will usually take place at a cemetery or crematorium that is owned by the local authority itself. In what way the next of kin can pay their last respects varies locally, and depends on the type of disposal.

5.5. SPECIAL INCOME SUPPORT

In Article 36 of the Dutch Participation Act – *de participatiewet* – funeral costs are described as 'special, inevitable costs of human existence'.[11] If the next of kin receive income support from the Dutch government and cannot afford

---

[8]Van Deutekom, H. & Van de Beek, K. (2017). *Gemeentelijke uitvaarten. Ontwikkelingen in 2016*. Ede: Christelijke Hogeschool Ede.

[9]Van Deutekom and Van de Beek (2017).

[10]See for instance, retrieved from https://www.ad.nl/nieuws/aantal-eenzame-uitvaarten-op-kosten-van-gemeente-stijgt~a577898c/. Accessed on March 5, 2019.

[11]Beleidsregels bijzondere bijstand, Article 36, Paragraph 1. Retrieved from https://zoek.officielebekendmakingen.nl/gmb-2015-47131.html. Accessed on December 11, 2018.

the funeral, they can apply for the Special Income Support Act – *bijzondere bijstand* – via the Social Services.[12] In this way, they – instead of the municipality – are enabled to organise the funeral of their significant other. Based on Nibud guidelines, the Social Services approve the funeral director's overview of estimated costs, and subsequently pay the funeral director. The next of kin receive a loan from the Social Services to pay for the costs, and will have to reimburse the state. They can do so by transferring a monthly amount. Alternatively, an amount may be withheld from people' social benefits. National data on the number of people receiving funeral funds under the Special Income Support Act is currently unavailable.

5.6. TECHNICAL CREMATION

When a technical cremation takes place, the deceased is removed to the crematorium and goes directly to the cremator. There is no service in the crematorium chapel. Sometimes, a few words might be spoken before the charge, either by the next of kin or by professionals, but typically there is no service at all. In terms of funeral costs, this can be a more attractive or necessary option. According to the Nibud guidelines a cremation service in the auditorium costs €1,250, whereas the expense of a technical cremation is estimated at €500.[13] Having no service, however, can also be part of the personalised funeral wishes of the deceased and

[12]Beleidsregels bijzondere bijstand, Article 36, Paragraph 1: To receive special support from the government, for instance to pay for a funeral, one must (1) live in the Netherlands, (2) be 18 years or older, (3) face real and inevitable expenses (4) that are caused by pressing or extraordinary circumstances, and (5) and that cannot be paid in an alternative manner. Those who receive income support typically meet the last criterion.
[13]Warnaar et al. (2017).

the next of kin.[14] Not having a service might suit the character of the deceased, or the service and condolences can be held at a different location, such as a restaurant, a church, a municipal hall, a pub or a school.

5.7. BABY AND CHILDREN'S FUNERALS

The Corpse Disposal Act applies to stillborn babies older than 24 weeks and those that have lived for more than 24 hours. They have to be registered, which includes obtaining a death certificate, and a burial or cremation must take place within six working days.[15] The Corpse Disposal Act does not apply to stillborn babies younger than 24 weeks. However, parents can register their stillborn child in the Personal Records Database Act (BRP) (see paragraph 3.3.2).[16]

The costs for a cremation or burial are often lower for the funerals of babies as well as children, but no national regulation exists. In recent years, a number of local trusts have been established to support parents emotionally, practically and financially. Often, these trusts are set up by people who themselves have experiences with stillbirth or losing a child, after whom the trust might be named. Since 2016, also a national expertise centre on stillbirth exists in the Netherlands.[17]

[14]Mathijssen, B. (2017a). *Making sense of death. Rituals practices and situational beliefs of the recently bereaved in the Netherlands.* Munster: Lit Verlag.
[15]Corpse Disposal Act, Article 2.
[16]Retrieved from https://www.eerstekamer.nl/wetsvoorstel/34882_wijziging_van_de_wet. Accessed on March 12, 2019.
[17]See https://www.stillelevens.nl for the expertise centre. For information on stillbirth rituals in the Netherlands see Peelen, J. (2012a). *Between birth and death. Rituals of pregnancy loss in the Netherlands.* Nijmegen: Radboud Universiteit. Or the Dutch summary: Peelen, J. (2012b). 'Tussen leven en dood. Rituelen rondom zwangerschapsverlies in Nederland'. *Yearbook for Ritual and Liturgical Studies.* 28, 259–265.

CHAPTER 6

A TYPICAL FUNERAL

6.1. DIVERSE AND TAILOR-MADE FUNERALS

Funerals in the Netherlands are tailor-made and personal. They are created in view of the wishes and lifestyles of those involved. These include the deceased, the next of kin, the wider circle of mourners, the funeral professionals, the religious or ritual experts, and the (religious) community. Opting for a religious or traditional funeral has become a personal choice, based on the importance of religion in the life of the deceased and the lives of those involved.[1] Rather than a pre-given, it is one of many options to choose from.

Because of vast regional differences and the country's significant religious and cultural diversity, it is impossible to describe *the* typical Dutch funeral. This not only holds in today's plural society, but also in the pillarised – thus

[1]Mathijssen, B. (2017a). *Making sense of death. Ritual practices and situational beliefs of the recently bereaved in the Netherlands.* Munster: Lit Verlag; Venbrux, E., Heessels, M. & Bolt, S. (eds.). (2008). *Rituele creativiteit: actuele veranderingen in de uitvaart en rouwcultuur in Nederland.* Zoetermeer: Meinema.

Table 6.1. Place of Death.

Place	Number of Deaths	Per Cent
Home	48,946	33
Hospital	35,765	24
Nursing home (*verpleeghuis*)	38,983	26
Elderly home (*verzorgingshuis*)	11,923	8
Elsewhere	13,380	9

Source: CBS. (2016). *Sterfte naar overlijden, nr 170183.*

plural – society of the past. Therefore, this chapter takes the diversity and the tailor-made character of funerals as a starting point. It describes some important aspects of arranging and performing the funeral. Moreover, it draws attention to a variety of actors that can become involved. Funerals in the Netherlands emerge from the picking and mixing of these elements and actors.

6.2. IMMEDIATELY FOLLOWING DEATH

When death occurs, the funeral must take place within six working days.[2] In the case of a Muslim or Jewish funeral, the funeral takes place as soon as possible. One-third of deaths in the Netherlands take place at home. It is also common for deaths to occur in hospital, in a nursing home or in an elderly home (Table 6.1). Depending on the type of death and the

[2]Corpse Disposal Act, article 16.

wishes of the dying person, a religious or civil celebrant or a spiritual caregiver may be present at the deathbed.

Immediately following death, a medical doctor has to visit the deceased to determine death and the cause of death. When someone passes away at home this is done by the general practitioner. In hospital or in a nursing home the treating physician performs the *lijkschouwing* – the 'witnessing of the corpse'. Alternatively, the municipal coroner can fulfil this job. If convinced that death has occurred as a result of a natural cause, the doctor signs a written declaration of death. This declaration is a prerequisite to conduct the funeral.[3]

In the Netherlands – as well as in Belgium and Germany – post-mortems are performed when a criminal offence is suspected. This differs, for instance, from the UK, where a post-mortem is conducted when the cause of death is unclear.[4] In practice, autopsy numbers are relatively low in the Netherlands and discussion exists whether the current process of inquiry is sufficient.[5] In 2014, 139,223 deaths occurred and 319 forensic sections took place in the Netherlands (0.2%). In Belgium, Germany and the UK, numbers were respectively 1,090 forensic sections on 109,034 deaths (1%), 17,367 on 868,356 deaths (2%), and 1,500 on 501,424 deaths (0.3%). In addition, 89,875 coroners' sections took place in the UK (10.4%).[6]

---

[3]Corpse Disposal Act, paragraph 1.

[4]Duijst-Heesters, W., Woudenberg-van den Broek, C. & Soerdjbalie-Maikoe, V. (2016). *De lijkschouw en sectie beschouwd. Een vergelijkend onderzoek naar systemen van lijkschouw en gerechtelijke sectie.* Den Haag: Nederlands Forensisch Instituut, Ministerie van Veiligheid en Justitie.

[5]See, for example, https://www.rtlnieuws.nl/gezondheid/artikel/3855281/lijkschouw-nederland-schiet-tekort-de-opleiding-was-een-veredelde-cursus. Accessed on April 13, 2019.

[6]Duijst-Heesters et al. (2016), p. 64.

In addition to the medical doctor, the family informs a funeral director. People are free to choose any funeral director, but the decision in part can be dictated by the funeral insurance. Using the funeral directing services of the insurance company comes with financial advantages, whereas choosing a different provider usually comes at an extra expense. As the family is not always aware of the deceased's funeral insurance, this can lead to challenges in practice.[7] The funeral director is contacted immediately after death because the funeral has to take place within a short time frame. The funeral director will visit the family of the deceased on the same or next day for an arrangement interview, and will make all practical funeral arrangements. In addition to the funeral director – or as an alternative – the family may inform a religious expert or community that death has occurred. In some cases, for example in the Orthodox Jewish community, the community has its own funeral directors who are in charge of making further arrangements. Alternatively, it is common for the funeral director to contact a religious or civil celebrant during the arrangement interview. Lastly, the next of kin are informed if they have not been present at the moment of death.

6.3. MAKING FUNERAL ARRANGEMENTS

The funeral is typically arranged by the funeral director and by the immediate family members, for example the spouse, (step) parent(s), child(ren) and/or sibling(s). Due to changing family compositions, the 'immediate family' category has become a dynamic one in recent decades. In addition to immediate family,

[7]Henselmans, M. (2017). *Laat je niet kisten door de commercie.* Oss: Genoeg.

close friends and the wider community may become involved in the funeral preparations. This is custom in particular religious communities, as well as in the case of an untimely death or the death of a public person. Examples are the active involvement of schoolmates or the local hockey or football club.

In practice, one member of the immediate family becomes the client (*opdrachtgever*) who carries the final responsibility for the funeral. This means that s/he signs off on the funeral choices that are being made, is responsible for the payment of the funeral and will have the custody of the cremated remains in the case of a cremation. In the absence of the next of kin, the executor or the municipality makes the arrangements.

6.3.1. Advance Funeral Wishes

In addition to making a will or testament, people make advance plans for their own funeral. Although no national numbers exist, research indicates that four out of five people have discussed their funeral wishes with significant others. About 30 per cent have also written down specific funeral wishes, either at home (on paper or a computer) or with an insurer or executor using a printed proforma or booklet.[8] In addition to personal information and written notes, these booklets and forms may contain information about:

- one's will and testament;
- one's executor;
- insurance policy;

[8]NL-Eyes. (2017). *Onderzoek voorstellen en voorbereiden. Onderzoeksverslag.* Haarlem: NL-Eyes. Retrieved from https://www.monuta.nl/sites/default/files/Onderzoeksverslag%20Voorstellen%20en%20voorbereiden.pdf

- medical record and donor codicil;
- preference for type of bodily disposal (burial; cremation; donation; next of kin decides)
- preference for cemetery or crematorium;
- preference for type of grave (general/private; other deceased) and maintenance;
- post-mortem care, dress;
- lying in state, open or closed coffin;
- public/private funeral;
- mourning and remembrance cards, advertisement in newspaper or online;
- coffin, flowers, transport;
- type of funeral, religion, celebrant, funeral director, speakers, music, recordings;
- end of funeral at auditorium or cemetery (e.g. what happens at the grave, cremator);
- food, drinks;
- tombstone, ash dispersal; and
- social media.

Funeral insurers, companies and a variety of associations support people in writing down their funeral wishes. Many do so for ideological reasons. They maintain that people themselves should be able to decide what happens to their bodies after death. Moreover, they believe that planning and writing down one's wishes supports the next of kin in organising the funeral. Financial motives also play a role. Advance funeral wishes can benefit companies as it may impact the purchasing of insurance policies and the choice for a funeral director. The funeral booklets and forms also have some formal status in the Netherlands, as the Corpse Disposal Act emphasises the importance of following the wishes of the deceased for both the next of kin and the local authority. Although a will or testament has a higher legal status, jurisprudence evidences that a booklet or form with funeral wishes has legal value and is taken into consideration in case of disputes or when the municipality organises and pays the funeral (see Section 3.3.3).

6.3.2. The Lonely Funeral: A Poetic Initiative

Some people pass away alone, unclaimed by friends or family. Bart FM Droog, the city poet of Groningen in 2001, came up with the idea to write and perform 'lonely funeral' poems for those without next of kin. From 2002 onwards, the initiative spread throughout the Netherlands and in 2006 the Lonely Funeral Association was founded – *Stichting De Eenzame Uitvaart* – as a local initiative in Amsterdam.[9] The poets of the 'lonely funeral movement' research the lives of the deceased, make tailor-made poems and read them out loud at the funeral. By doing so they bring a special salute to those who passed away alone. They remind us what it means to be human and critique the social neglect during their lives.

Similar initiatives can be found for others who have been abandoned or rejected by society, like the homeless or those with addictions or psychiatric problems. Volunteers, religious experts and spiritual care professionals play a role in their funerals or organise memorial services. They not only bring humanity, care and dignity to the deceased, but

[9]On the association's website more information, including the poems that have been written at funerals in Amsterdam, can be found. Retrieved from http://www.eenzameuitvaart.nl

also to the living who – due to problems – might have no place to mourn.

6.4. ARRANGEMENTS WITH THE FUNERAL DIRECTOR

The funeral director visits the family at home to arrange the funeral on the day death has occurred, or the day after. The arrangement interview generally lasts for three hours, during which all practical matters are discussed regarding the care for the body of the deceased, the funeral preparations, the funeral and the bodily disposal.

6.4.1. Type of Funeral

After condolences, introductions, and explaining the aim of the arrangement interview, the funeral director starts with discussing the type of the funeral. Will there be a cremation or a burial? Will the service be non-religious, Christian, Muslim, Humanist, Javanese, Caribbean, Ghanaian, Surinamese or Chinese? These decisions impact all other preparations. Also at an earlier stage, they determine which funeral director visits the family. Moreover, in some groups the community might organise the funeral instead of the funeral director.

6.4.2. Place, Time and Length of the Service

During the interview the place, time and length of the funeral have to be discussed and the crematorium or cemetery has to be booked. If applicable, also a church, mosque, restaurant or other auditorium space must be arranged. This is done via telephone by the funeral director during the interview with the next of kin.

6.4.3. Mourning Cards and Death Notices

Relatives, friends, colleagues and acquaintances are typically notified of the death and are invited to the funeral. This is often done via mourning cards: special postcards or letters that are send by mail, and that can be recognised by a black rim on the envelope. The mourning cards are written during the arrangement interview with the funeral director, and the design, texts and images are often based on templates (Image 6.1). A draft of the mourning card is usually printed and read out loud during the interview to check spelling, rhythm and tone. By doing so, the cards can be distributed on time before the funeral. Today, email and social media are increasingly used. It is also common to place a death notice in the local or national newspaper, although this practice is declining. The cost of a set number mourning cards is typically embedded in the funeral insurance.

6.4.4. The Coffin or Shroud

The next of kin choose a coffin during the arrangement interview. A wide selection of possibilities is provided by the funeral director, varying from traditional to highly personalised and eco-friendly designs. Whereas it is possible for people to search for a coffin elsewhere or online, this is not common due to the time pressures. Also, people's funeral insurance might discourage this.

Using a coffin is common, but is not a legal requirement in the Netherlands. Rules do exist concerning the casing of the

Image 6.1. An Example of a Contemporary Mourning Card, with Fictional Information, Based on Digital Templates.

Veel fijne herinneringen
verzachten ons verdriet.
Voorgoed uit ons midden
maar vergeten doen wij niet.

Dankbaar voor alles wat zij voor ons heeft betekend,
geven wij kennis van het overlijden van

Brenda Venhorst

Geboren 27 maart 1985 te Venlo
Overleden 01 januari 2019 te Groningen

Peter en Claudia
Sjoukje en Danny
Julia en Nick
Hanneke
Eric en Anne

Correspondentie-adres:
Familie Venhorst-Mathijssen
Hoofdstraat 123
9723 PB Groningen

Brenda is thuis. Bezoektijden dinsdag 3 januari van 15 tot 17 uur en woensdag 4 januari vanaf 12 uur.

De avondwake is op donderdag 5 januari om 19.00 uur bij uitvaartondernemer Nissen, Noordeinde 187 te Groningen. Na de avondwake is er gelegenheid tot condoleren.

De uitvaartdienst zal plaatsvinden op vrijdag 6 januari om 15 uur in crematorium Ommeland Aan de Crematoriumlaan 1 te Groningen.

body. When the deceased is transported during the funeral process, and to the cremator or grave, this must happen in a hygienic way. Also, the materials used to envelop the body should be biodegradable. For instance, no plastic lining is allowed in the coffin. This requirement does not extend to the clothes of the deceased.

Although it is not a legal requirement, crematoria usually prescribe the use of a coffin or coffin-like structure. Reasons for this are the health and safety of the crematorium employees, and the workings of the cremator. In the case of burial, use of a shroud is permitted. Shroud burials became legal in 1997 after an amendment of The Corpse Disposal Act particularly to accommodate the Muslim community in the Netherlands. Shrouds are also increasingly used as a green alternative.

A basic coffin is typically included in the funeral insurance, and personalised coffins and shrouds are available at an extra expense. The specific costs depend on the type of coffin or shroud that is chosen. Whereas people can opt for a coffin or shroud that is not provided by the funeral insurance company, this often is a costlier option – particularly in the case of in-kind insurance (see Section 5.3).

6.4.5. Flowers

Floral tributes are discussed during the interview and arrangements are either made with the funeral director or directly with the local florist, who is often less expensive. In addition to the flowers of the immediate family, other mourners might order flowers at their local florist. The florist brings the flowers to the funeral home, where they are held in a special storage room. Some flowers, for instance a family bouquet, may be placed in the mourning chamber with the deceased on the day of the funeral, or the evening before. This could accompany the wake or the closing of the coffin. Alternatively, special flowers may be bought to decorate the mourning room. On the day of the funeral, the flowers travel along in the hearse with the deceased.

During the funeral, the flower bouquet of the immediate family is usually placed on top of the coffin and the floral tributes of the nearest and dearest mourners are placed around the coffin. Also, they are used to decorate the auditorium. A ribbon is often attached to the flowers, depicting a wish or thank you to the deceased and/or the names of those sending the tribute. After the funeral the flowers are either placed on the grave of the deceased, on the graves or memorials of other deceased kith and kin, or on a special floral tribute area at the crematorium or cemetery grounds.

It is increasingly common for the next of kin to ask the wider community of mourners to not bring flowers, but to make a donation to charity instead. The specific charity is typically related to the life and/or death of the deceased.

6.4.6. Music

Funeral music is extensively discussed among the next of kin. It is mentioned by both funeral professionals and a variety of celebrants, and the next of kin are invited to think about the meaning of music for themselves and their deceased. The composition and the lyrics of funeral music tell a story. It may be a favourite song, a reminder of shared and treasured experiences, or a reference to personal traits of the deceased.[10]

Although funerals have become rather personalised, specific songs and tunes reappear. This is well captured by the existence of the Funeral Top 10, a list of the most popular funeral songs which currently includes Andrea Bocelli's *Time to Say Goodbye*, Eric Clapton's *Tears in Heaven* and Stef Bos' *Papa*. Many crematoria have a local Funeral Top 10, and many funeral companies show them on their websites or on platforms like Spotify to help people to make a suitable choice for their own funeral or the funeral of a significant other.[11]

---

[10]Mathijssen (2017a), pp. 70–72.

[11]For a study on funeral music in the Netherlands, see Bruin-Mollenhorst, J. & Hoondert, M. (2018). 'Musical media in Dutch crematoria, 1914–present'. *Thanatos*. 7 (1), 6–31.

6.4.7. Koffietafel

It is common to have a social gathering together with all or a selection of the funeral participants after the funeral ceremony. This is called the *koffietafel* (lit. coffee-table) and typically includes food and drinks. Traditionally, it consists of coffee and cake – hence the name – but today lunches, dinners or receptions with beers and *bitterballen* are no exception. Historically, the coffee-table tends to be more elaborate in the south of Netherlands than it is in the north. The *koffietafel* can be held at different locations, for instance at the restaurant facilities or café in the crematorium building or at the cemetery grounds (see 8.6.5). If the location is part of the crematorium or cemetery, the funeral director books the restaurant and catering during the arrangement interview. In view of time restrictions, costs, atmosphere or the importance of a particular pub or restaurant for the deceased and/or the bereaved, people may also organise their 'coffee-table' at a different location. This is arranged by the immediate family. In some communities and families, the social gatherings after the funeral continue for multiple days at home or within the community.

6.5. ARRANGEMENTS WITH THE RELIGIOUS OR CIVIL CELEBRANT

In addition to the funeral director, a religious or civil celebrant might be involved in the funeral. This option is typically discussed during the practical arrangement interview and, if decided upon, the funeral director will check the availability of the celebrant. Subsequently, the immediate family makes an appointment with the celebrant for a separate interview to prepare the content of the funeral ceremony. This interview takes place within the next few days. In the case of a Muslim or Jewish funeral, the arrangements with the religious community have already been made in view of the obligation to bury as soon as possible.

The choice for a type of celebrant is based on the worldview of those involved. It is based on the lifestyle of the deceased and the bereaved. For instance, the specific religious community s/he was a member of, or particular values or traits. It is increasingly common for the next of kin to organise the content of the ceremony themselves, often under the sole guidance of the funeral director.

6.5.1. Minister, Pastor or Priest

In the case of a Christian funeral a minister, pastor or priest will conduct the funeral and will visit the next of kin for an interview as regards the content of the ceremony. In some cases, a pastoral worker or ritual coach may be involved instead (see 6.5.6). The deceased and the bereaved can be well-acquainted with the Christian celebrant and the church, but this is not a given.[12] Due to declining church membership and the large dispersion of family members throughout the country, the next of kin are increasingly unfamiliar with the local church. When people move to a nursing or elderly home, they may also loosen ties with the former church community for reasons of distance and health. In such cases, it is

[12]For a description of Roman Catholic and Protestant funeral preparations, see Mathijssen (2017a). For a study on Dutch Roman Catholic Funerals at the beginning of the twenty-first century, see Quartier, T. (2007). *Bridging the gaps. An empirical study of Catholic funeral rites.* Münster: Lit Verlag.

possible that the celebrant does not know the deceased and/ or the next of kin.

During the interview with the minister (for Protestant Churches, for example the Dutch Reformed Church or the Reformed Churches in the Netherlands) or the priest (for Roman Catholic Churches) the funeral liturgy is prepared. Choices are made as regards the type of service, the readings, the music and so on. These are arranged within the liturgy of the denomination and the celebrant involved.

6.5.2. Imam and Volunteers

In the case of a Muslim funeral, an Imam is typically involved.[13] Where traditional Imams are either the ones leading in prayer (Sunni tradition) or the spiritual leader of the community (Shia), in the Dutch migration context they are best described as professional Imams who are leading a local mosque community. The vast majority of mosques in the Netherlands are founded by a variety of Turkish-Islamic and Moroccan-Islamic organisations to serve their specific communities, and Imams are appointed by the mosque organisations and generally come directly from Turkey or Morocco where they were trained.[14] Professional Imams in the Netherlands do not only lead the congregation in prayer but also take on many pastoral duties and play a leading role in

[13]For a description of Muslim funeral preparations see Venhorst, C. (2013). *Muslims ritualising death in the Netherlands. Death rites in a small town context.* Münster: Lit Verlag; Dessing, N. (2001). *Rituals of birth, circumcision, marriage and death among Muslims in the Netherlands.* Leuven: Peeters.

[14]Retrieved from http://polderislam.nl/achtergronden/moslims-en-islamitische-instituties-in-nederland/islamitische-koepelorganisaties-en-contactorganen#inleiding. Accessed on April 14, 2019.

education on and performance of Islamic rites of passage from birth to death – something they typically did not do in their country of origin.

Being Muslim in a minority context comes with a lot of uncertainties and a fear for ritual failure, and the Imam is expert in matters concerning the correct ritual practice. He is involved in the ritual cleansing and shrouding of the deceased (either performing or guiding it), performing the Islamic funeral prayer and the burial. To perform the ritual cleansing properly and respectfully a single person is not sufficient, and because of strict gender regulations a deceased woman can only be washed by women. Local community members, volunteers at a mosque and employees of Islamic funeral companies perform the ritual washing of the deceased in the Netherlands (see Section 6.6.1).

6.5.3. Chevra Kadisha

The Jewish community in the Netherlands is small and diverse. Within Judaism it is the duty of the next of kin as well as the wider community to arrange the funeral of the deceased. In practice this wider community – the *Chevra Kadisha* – usually exists of volunteers.[15] A rabbi may officiate the funeral service, but this is not a requirement nor standard practice. Rather, there is a (orthodox) Jewish funeral association in the Netherlands, called *het Joods Begrafeniswezen*, that conducts the burials of the Ashkenazi and Portuguese communities in the region of Amsterdam.

[15]For a description of Jewish funeral practices see Martel, S. (2004). *Sterk als de dood. Sterven en rouw in joods perspectief*. Amsterdam: Eburon Uitgeverij.

The city also has a Jewish Hospice.[16] Most contemporary Jewish burials are conducted at the cemeteries of Muiderberg and Ouderkerk aan de Amstel.

6.5.4. Pandit

A small and diverse community exists in the Netherlands of people who identify as Hindu. The largest group of Hindus are the *Hindoestanen*, who find their origins in Surinam. Many of them moved to the Netherlands after the 1975 independence (see Sections 1.2 and 1.3). Additionally, there are Hindus from India, South Africa, Mauritius and Uganda.

The Pandit plays an important role in Hindu deathbed, funerary and ash disposal practices (see Section 8.7.4). He or she reads the Vedic texts, sings and prays with the next of kin and funeral participants. The specific Hindu denomination, *Sanatan Dharm* or *Arya Samaadj*, determines which funerary practices are performed and also influences the length of the service.[17]

6.5.5. Humanistic Celebrant

The humanistic celebrant assists the next of kin in the preparations and performance of the funeral. S/he is associated to the Humanist Association – founded in 1946 – and works from a humanist frame of reference. This means that

[16]For information about the Jewish hospice, see https://www.joodshospiceimmanuel.nl/

[17]Parry, J. P. (1994). *Death in Banaras*. Cambridge: Cambridge University Press.

the human being takes centre stage within an immanent frame, in the here and now.[18]

6.5.6. Ritual Coach or Civil Celebrant

In the last two decades a new group of ritual experts has emerged in the Netherlands – often named ritual coaches or ritual guides, but also referred to as civil celebrants, funeral speakers or funeral coaches.[19] Like the humanistic celebrant, the ritual coach offers an alternative to the traditional religious funeral expert. S/he works independently and assists the next of kin in making the funeral content. In this process they typically adapt to the worldview of the deceased and next of kin, as well as using their own frame of reference. The ritual coach generally conducts the funeral ceremony or plays other significant roles in the funeral performance.[20]

6.6. THE CARE OF THE DECEASED

Once the medical doctor has visited the deceased and has determined natural death, the deceased will receive post-mortem care (*afleggen*): the body will be washed and dressed. This usually happens at the funeral home, but the deceased can also receive post-mortem care in the hospital or in the

[18]Brabers, J., Markx, S. & Reinders, W. (2006). *Uitvaartbegeleiding op humanistische grondslag*. Amsterdam: Humanistisch Verbond; Engelke, M. (2015). 'The coffin question: death and materiality in humanist funerals'. *Material Religion*. 11(1), 26–48.

[19]This variety results from the changing and unfixed status of the celebrants' roles. There are vast regional differences as regards their job title and their popularity.

[20]For a detailed description of the work of the ritual coach and civil celebrant, see Mathijssen (2017a).

nursing home. The care is typically given by two people, for instance mortuary technicians (*overledenenverzorger*) or nurses, and the process follows a protocol. The protocol is not legally binding, but follows good and common practice. Mortuaries, elderly homes, hospices and hospitals therefore typically have a protocol in place.[21]

Before the washing starts, four things are checked. First, the deceased's donor codicil is consulted. If the deceased is registered as a donor, this could impact the process. Second, the religious beliefs of the deceased determine the procedure of post-mortem care. In the case of a Muslim death, for example, the protocol is a different one and the ritual washing is typically done by community or family members of the same sex. Third, the immediate family are consulted as they might want to assist in the washing and dressing of their deceased. The funeral director enquires about their wishes during the arrangement interview. Moreover, the next of kin have to give permission for conducting certain post-mortem practices, such as the closing of the mouth and the replacement of dentures. Fourth, if the deceased has a pacemaker and will be cremated, this must be removed before the further washing and dressing.[22] The next of kin will be notified (and consulted) about this.

The washing of the deceased follows a typical order. Before the body is washed, the clothes and jewellery are removed. Using warm water and a washcloth, the body is

[21]An example of such a protocol can be found at www.overledenezorg-pro.nl, accessed on May 11, 2019. At the uitvaart.nl channel on YouTube, videos about caring for the deceased can also be found.

[22]In the current discussions about the Corpse Disposal Act, it is discussed whether legislation should also include the removal of a pacemaker in the case of a burial (Roundtable discussion, House of Representatives, The Hague, 11 April 2019).

cleaned and the hair is washed. Also, the nails are cut. During the washing process the loss of fluids – which results from the absence of muscle tension after death – is taken into consideration. The bladder is often emptied preventively by pressing it. After washing, the cavities from which moisture loss can occur are usually sealed. A diaper is often also used. After the washing of the body, the eyes and mouth are closed. The eyes are closed with a sticker or small cap that is placed under the eyelid. The mouth is closed with a small pad under the chin. Alternatively, it sometimes is closed with a single suture.

Subsequently the deceased is dressed. The immediate bereaved usually choose clothes for the deceased as well as jewellery or other objects, such as glasses. The deceased may also have conveyed wishes in this regard. Often, the goal is to make people look as natural as possible. Also, people want their deceased to look at his/her best out of respect. Moreover, particular characteristics of the deceased might be emphasised through the choice of clothes, for example, a football player wearing his football shirt.

Finally, the hair and make-up are done, typically in the way the deceased had done during life. A cream may be applied on the skin and the colour of the skin may me be made less pale. Sometimes a picture of the deceased can help to visualise the preferred post-mortem appearance, and this can assist the mortuary technicians in the process.

Embalming is illegal in the Netherlands, with the exception of the royal family. The practice of thanatopraxy became legal in 2010. This is a method to conserve the body for a short period of time – ca. 10 days or until the day of the funeral – without the need for cooling facilities. Like embalming, the body is preserved. Unlike embalming, the conservation period is short and therefore a smaller amount of formalin is used (0.5%).

6.6.1. Ritual Washing

Dutch funeral homes try to facilitate specific requirements needed to perform the ritual washing. Some groups perform a ritual cleansing or purification of the deceased, as prescribed by their religious or cultural tradition. Muslims (*Ghusl*) and Jews (*Tahara*) perform a similar cleansing ritual carried out by specially trained and gender-specific volunteers or ritual specialists. The washing can be conducted at the funeral directors' premises or at community facilities. In case of a deceased Muslim, the closest gender-specific relatives are strongly encouraged to participate in the ritual washing. The Surinamese Creole community undertakes a very elaborate and secretive washing ceremony (*wasi dede, dinariwroko*) performed by the *dinari*.[23] Becoming a *dinari* is an honorary function to which one must be invited and for which one is extensively trained.

6.6.2. Viewing the Deceased

In the period before the funeral, the deceased can be installed at home or at the funeral home. The next of kin might wish to visit the deceased, and arrangements for this are made during the interview with the funeral director.

In the funeral home the deceased can either stay in a cooled storage room or in a private chamber. When the deceased resides in the cooled storage room, the family must make an appointment with the funeral home to visit him or her. Before the appointment the deceased is removed to a

---

[23]Van der Pijl, Y. (2007). *Levende-doden. Afrikaans-Surinaamse percepties, praktijken en rituelen rondom dood en rouw*, Bronnen voor de studie van Suriname, deel 27. Amsterdam: IBS, Rozenberg Publishers.

mourning room (*rouwkamer*), where the bereaved can visit and view the deceased. The family can make as many appointments as they would like. It is common to combine (one of) the appointment(s) with a wake or condolence visit. In the southern part of the Netherlands, the wake used to be a church remembrance service preceding the funeral. Today, it is typically a gathering at the funeral home or at home. It lasts for about an hour in the evening before the funeral. The wake allows people to say goodbye to the deceased before the coffin is closed. It also offers an opportunity to close the coffin, which is usually done by the closest family members.[24]

Alternatively, the family can rent a private mourning room in the funeral home. The deceased resides in this room until the funeral takes place, and the bereaved can access the room 24/7 with a separate key. They can fully decorate the room and use it in any way they like. If desired, they can invite family and friends to join them. Also, a wake can be organised in the private mourning room.

Traditionally the deceased would be kept at home until the day of or the day before the funeral. This practice diminished due to the professionalisation of death, but is becoming popular again. The deceased can be placed in bed, in a coffin or on a static bier or shelf (*opbaarplank*) and cooling facilities must be used, unless thanatopraxy has been applied to the body. Special cooling equipment exists to use at home. Also at home, the temporal resting place of the deceased is often decorated by the bereaved. By installing the deceased at home, the family has the opportunity to say goodbye and to stay together with

[24]It is also possible to close the coffin just before the funeral service, and to allow all mourners to view the deceased. Also, open coffin funerals are possible in the Netherlands. The coffin is then closed at the end of the service. Particular religious groups opt for an open coffin, but the practice is also increasingly common at 'non-religious' funeral services.

the deceased in a familiar environment. Also other people, such as friends, family members and neighbours, tend to visit the home in the period before the funeral.

6.7. THE DAY OF THE FUNERAL

6.7.1. Dress

On the day of the funeral, the immediate family and other funeral participants dress in clothes that they see fit for the occasion. Black or dark colours were custom in the past, but this has changed since the 1980s. Dress today is adjusted to the wishes and the lifestyle – socio-economic class, hobbies, friends, religion, cultural background – of the deceased and the next of kin. This can also include the dress of the celebrant, especially when s/he does not represent a formal (religious) institution.

6.7.2. Travel to the Funeral Service

At the day of the funeral, the deceased is removed from the funeral home – or the alternative place of residence – to the location of the funeral service. A hearse is typically used for this. In Dutch the hearse used to be called a 'corpse-vehicle' (*lijkwagen*) and is today typically referred to as a 'mourning-vehicle' (*rouwauto*). Based on the wishes of the deceased and the next of kin, the hearse can drive via the house of the deceased to bring a salute. At the cemetery or crematorium premises there typically is a special parking place for the hearse, and a separate entrance for the deceased.

The immediate family may form a cortege behind the hearse, using their own cars or using 'follow-vehicles'. These are special vehicles in the style of the hearse that include a driver. Some of the nearest and dearest bereaved may also join the cortege in their own vehicles. As funerals have become increasingly informal, the use of formal follow-vehicles has become less common. The hearse on duty – when it is part of a funeral procession – can be recognised by two black, white-rimmed, triangular flags at the front of the car. The three white stripes on the flags are a relatively new sight. Since 1 July 2010, they have replaced a white cross (Image 6.2). Today many alternatives exist to the traditional black hearse. There are pink or colourfully decorated Cadillacs, classic cars and buses that transport both the deceased and the mourners. Of course, it is possible also to transport the deceased by bicycle or a special funeral-bicycle (Image 6.3). The possibilities are endless.

Image 6.2. A Hearse, Characterised by the Triangular Flags with Three White Stripes at the Front.

Source: Van der Lans & Busscher Staatsievervoer and Straver Mobility.

Image 6.3. A Funeral Bicycle, Used to Transport the Deceased to the Cemetery or Crematorium.

Source: Van der Lans & Busscher Staatsievervoer and Straver Mobility.

Once the deceased has arrived at the funeral location, s/he is brought to the specific auditorium or room for the funeral service. The deceased is generally removed from the hearse by professionals, using a bier, and the next of kin can assist in this process. It is common practice at crematoria to place the deceased in the auditorium before the start of the service. This is also when the space is decorated (6.7.4). Alternatively, the deceased can be carried into the place for the funeral service by the next of kin or by professional bearers as the funeral starts. Carrying the deceased into church is part of many Christian funeral services, and the immediate family may form a cortege behind the deceased. It is also common to carry the deceased in Islamic practice.

6.7.3. The Place of the Funeral

Funeral services can be held at a variety of locations. The most common location today is the crematorium (see Chapter 8). In the case of a burial, the auditorium at the cemetery premises might be used (see Chapter 7). Also, services can be held in the local church, in the mosque, or in a community centre, theatre, restaurant or auditorium space. People are increasingly using other locations than the traditional crematorium, cemetery or church.

6.7.4. Decorating the Funeral Location

The funeral location is typically decorated in view of the wishes of the deceased and the immediate family. The extent to which the funeral can be decorated depends on the specific location. Typically, there are fewer possibilities in the case of a traditional mass in church, and more possibilities in the case of a 'non-religious' service in a local restaurant.

The funeral director ensures that all decorations are delivered on time and are in place when the funeral starts. S/he often decorates the location together with the staff, e.g. the crematorium or restaurant employees, and with the immediate family themselves. Typical examples of decorations are a picture of the deceased, candles and flowers, but also more extravagant or personalised items may be used. Examples are paintings, statues, motorcycles or bicycles, plants, PowerPoint presentations, videos or objects relating to a favourite football club or city. If it suits the deceased, the location might also be dressed in a minimal or sober fashion.

In the case of a religious service, religious symbols are often used (Image 6.4). Furthermore, some decorations might be forbidden. Orthodox Protestant groups might not permit

Image 6.4. Religious Symbols at a Dutch Crematorium.

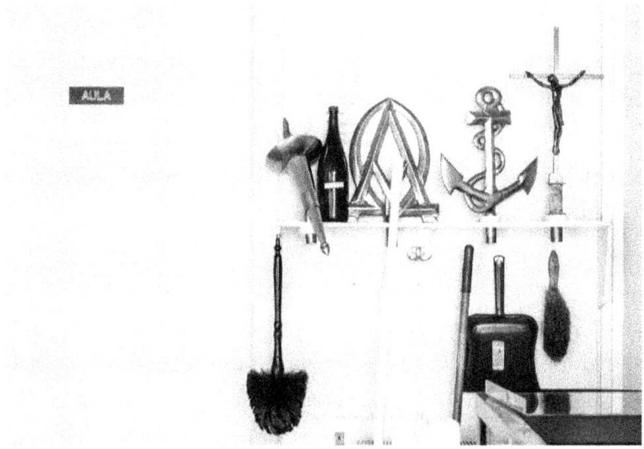

Source: Photograph by Claudia Venhorst.

the use of candles, and at Muslims funerals pictures might be prohibited.

6.7.5. Orders of Service

In ecclesial funeral services, an order of service is typically printed for the funeral participants to follow. At other funerals, it seldom plays a role. Orders of service are used for the preparation of the funeral, and the celebrant often has a written order of service. This is typically used as a script and handed to the next of kin as a memento after the funeral.

6.7.6. Attending the Funeral

Funerals in the Netherlands are public events, unless the announcement of death or mourning card states otherwise.

This means that, theoretically, funerals are open to everyone. Who should attend the funeral in practice strongly depends on the type of death, and on cultural customs. Family, friends, colleagues, (known) neighbours and members of one's (religious) community are likely to attend the funeral. When death is unexpected or untimely, the group of funeral participants is usually larger in number and younger in age.

The deceased and/or the next of kin can decide to organise a private funeral. It then becomes an invitation-only event. Private funerals may be organised when a public figure has passed away. It is also more common when the cause of death or family relations are in some way problematic.

6.7.7. The Funeral Service

Funeral services in the Netherlands are tailor-made in view of the personal, cultural and religious preferences and obligations of the deceased and the mourners. As people's lifestyles have become more varied, so have their funerals. As a result, it is no longer self-evident that a funeral is recognisable and meaningful to all attending mourners. This is especially the case when the attendees form a heterogeneous group, for instance because of religious diversity, decreased numbers of formal religious observance or increased generational or social differences. In practice, this can result in challenges and in funerals that are perceived as inappropriate. In response to the increased heterogeneity and pluralism, mourners and funeral professionals are compelled to search for ways to reinvent funeral services.

In today's funeral services the celebration and remembrance of the life of the deceased increasingly takes centre stage.[25] People's personal wishes and preferences determine the type of funeral service – whether it is a cremation or a burial, whether it is a religious or non-religious service – and its content – the speeches, eulogy, life story, objects, pictures, religious readings, prayers, recitations, clothes, videos, (popular) music, hymns, poetry and/or decorations. Moreover, it has become common to combine different types of funeral or memorial services – for instance a traditional mass in church with a personal remembrance service – to meet the diverse needs of the next of kin. (Religious) Institutions and traditions play a significant role when they are deemed important by the deceased and the mourners, and are increasingly shaped and interpreted on the basis of the lives of those involved.

6.7.7.1. Christian Funeral Framework

Christian funerals typically follow a liturgy that is shaped and structured in view of the particular denominational tradition. Roman Catholics follow a prescribed and rather strict funeral liturgy. Protestants use the liturgical formats of the Protestant Church in the Netherlands, or their specific denomination or local church.[26] They typically have more freedom to add, remove or adjust liturgical elements. The following overview gives a general indication of the ritual elements in Christian funerals.

---

[25]Venbrux, E., Peelen J. & Altena M. (2009). 'Going Dutch: individualisation, secularisation and changes in death rites'. *Mortality*. 14 (2), 97–101; Wojtkowiak, J., Rutjens, B. & Venbrux, E. (2010). 'Meaning making and death in a secular society: a Dutch survey study'. *Archive for the Psychology of Religion*. 32, 363–373; Wouters, C. (2002). 'The quest for new rituals in dying and mourning: changes in the we-I balance'. *Body & Society*. 8 (1), 81–166, 1–2.

[26]Mathijssen, B. (2013). 'Pastors and relatives: enacting Protestant and Catholic funeral liturgies in the Netherlands'. In E. Venbrux et. al. (eds.). *Changing European death ways*. Münster: Lit Verlag, 213–239.

Roman Catholic Funeral (Eucharist)[a]	Protestant Church in the Netherlands Funeral (Prayer Service)[b]
Opening rite	Entering the church
Entering the church (mourners first, then the deceased, officials, family)	Word of welcome and introduction
Word of welcome and introduction	
[Eulogy]	Personal remembrance
	Choir or instrumental music
Service of the Word	Reading holy scripture
Reading holy scripture (1OT)	Readings [including singing]
[Singing psalms]	
Homilies	Sermon
Intercession	Choir or instrumental music
	[Confession]
[Offertory – collection of money]	
Eucharist	
Prayer	Prayer
[Word of thanks and farewell]	Word of thanks
	Intercession
Absolution	
[Blessing]	
Leaving the Church	Leaving the Church
Music (choir)	Music (choir)
Cemetery or Crematorium	Cemetery or Crematorium
	[Confession]
	Prayer or the Lord
	Blessing
Social gathering	Social gathering

Source: [a]Nationale Raad voor Liturgie. (1976). *Liturgie van de sacramenten en andere kerkelijke vieringen*. De Uitvaartliturgie. Hilversum: Gooi & Sticht. [b]Commissie Dienstboek. (1987). *Liturgie in dagen van rouw. Proeven voor de eredienst. Aflevering I.* Leidschendam/Leusden.

6.7.7.2. Muslim Funeral Framework

The most important elements of a Muslim funeral are the ritual washing and shrouding of the deceased, the funeral prayer and the burial.[27] In the Netherlands the ritual washing of the deceased can be of extreme importance, especially when the deceased is repatriated to the country of origin.[28] It is often the last opportunity to pay one's respects and to fulfil one's religious obligations.

A Muslim funeral

Ritual washing and shrouding of the deceased

Entering the mosque

Reading holy scripture

Ṣalāt al-Janāzah (funeral prayer or *du'â*) in silence, except for the *takbîrs* and *taslîm* that are spoken by the Imam)

Burial (at cemetery in the Netherlands or in country of origin after repatriation)

Social gathering

6.7.7.3. Non-ecclesial Funeral Framework

Non-ecclesial funerals typically do not follow the ritual orders of religious traditions. However, we can observe repetitive patterns in the structure and elements of these funerals.[29] The content is usually tailored in view of the wishes of the deceased and the mourners. As the framework below indicates, there often is a combination of speeches and music before the actual cremation or burial takes place.

---

[27]Dessing, N. (2001). *Rituals of birth, circumcision, marriage and death among Muslims in the Netherlands*. Leuven: Peeters.
[28]Venhorst (2013, 31ff).
[29]Mathijssen (2017a).

A non-ecclesial funeral

Entering the auditorium

Word of welcome to all mourners, especially the immediate family

Opening words about the deceased

Speech, life story of the deceased, eulogy by a family member, colleague, friend, expert

Music

Speech, poem, prayer, etc. by a family member, colleague, friend
Music
Poem

Word of thanks and farewell

Music and leaving auditorium

Cremation or burial

Social gathering

6.7.8. Committal, Burial and Cremation

The committal is the moment at the end of the funeral service when the body is removed from view. In the case of a cremation, the funeral director and the mourners typically walk by the coffin at the end of the service to pay their last respects before they leave the auditorium. They do so in a queue, one by one or in pairs. The closest family members stay behind to pay their last respects together in private, before also they leave the auditorium. The deceased is removed from the auditorium to the cremator room by staff when all mourners have left the auditorium. Alternatively, it is common for the closest family members to join the deceased in the cremator room. Here, they pay their last respects, and they are likely to witness and initiate the charge under the guidance of the cremator operator (see 8.6.4).

In the case of a burial it is common for all or a select group of mourners to join the deceased at the graveside. The coffin is removed from the chapel and carried by bearers or by immediate family members. Alternatively, the coffin is placed on a removable bier, or the catafalque can function as a bier to remove the deceased to the cemetery. At the graveside, words or prayers can be said by the next of kin or by the celebrant or funeral director. This can happen before and/or during the lowering of the coffin in the grave. The lowering of the coffin is common, but not standard. Some mourners prefer that the coffin stays above the earth when they pay their last respects. In those cases, the coffin is lowered into the grave after people have left the cemetery.

When the immediate family chooses to witness the lowering of the coffin into the grave, this can be done by hand or automatically. The celebrant, funeral director and/or family may cast earth on the coffin. Alternatively, they may cast small flowers or leave a note. In some traditions other objects may also be placed in the grave. Subsequently, all mourners present at the cemetery are invited to cast a handful of earth on the coffin to pay their last respects before they leave the graveside.

The grave is backfilled by the cemetery staff when everyone has left the cemetery grounds. (A selection of) The floral tributes are placed on top, together with a sign that shows the name of the deceased and the dates and place(s) of birth and death. In some communities people themselves assist in or do the backfilling.

6.7.9. Digital Recording

Many funeral locations – with the exception of some religious buildings – offer the option to make use of digital equipment: music, video, PowerPoint and audio and video recording. The next of kin can order a video recording of the funeral, which they receive after the service. In some cases, especially at crematoria, live-stream services are also provided. This is used when family members or friends cannot attend the funeral, for instance due to illness or to being abroad. At auditoria and crematoria, one can observe signs informing mourners that a video recording might be made of the funeral service.

People can also hire a photographer to record the funeral service. Alternatively, people can make photographs themselves with a camera or a mobile phone. In some cases, this is common and accepted practice. In other cases, whether taking pictures is 'respectful' is subject to debate.

6.7.10. Remembrance or Prayer Cards

It is common for the funeral participants to receive a remembrance or prayer card – a *gedachtenisprentje* or *bidprentje* – when they leave the auditorium at the end of the funeral service. This is a small card with the name of the deceased, the date and place of birth, and a small part of the life story, eulogy and/or a poem (Images 6.5 and 6.6). There might also be a picture. The card functions as a small memento of the deceased.

The prayer cards find their origin in Roman Catholic funerary traditions, and the custom is therefore most common in the south of the Netherlands. As a result of the changing role of religion, the prayer cards have gradually been transformed into remembrance cards, which are a secular alternative that can be found throughout the country.

Image 6.5. Typical Mourning Card 1951.

WILT IN UWE GEBEDEN GEDENKEN

WILHELMINA KLEIN

echtgenote van

HERMANUS JOHANNES VENHORST

Zij werd de 28ste Juli 1886 te Megchelen geboren en overleed de 30ste April 1951, voorzien van de H.H. Sacramenten der Stervenden. De 2de Mei d.a.v. werd zij op het R.K. Kerkhof te Megchelen begraven en verwacht daar de Opstanding.

Jezus zeide tot Martha: Ik ben de verrijzenis en het leven; wie in Mij gelooft, zal leven, ook al is hij gestorven; en wie leeft en in Mij gelooft, zal niet sterven in eeuwigheid. Gelooft gij dit?

Ja, Heer, wij geloven U en het is ons een grote troost nu wij onze Moeder ten grave dragen, dat Gij aan allen die in U geloven, het eeuwige leven schenkt, en dat Gij eenmaal ook haar lichaam dat wij nu aan de schoot der aarde toevertrouwen, heerlijk en onbederfelijk, in jeugd en kracht weer ten leven zult wekken.

En mogen wij dat niet vast verhopen van deze vrome vrouw en goede moeder, die elf kinderen het leven schonk. Drie van hen kozen de religieuse staat en de anderen bouwen op het voorbeeld van vader en moeder weer nieuwe christelijke gezinnen op. Droefheid vervult hen nu, nu zij afscheid van haar nemen, maar zij worden getroost door de gedachte, dat er voor hen een weerzien is bij God. En de gedachte aan hun lieve moeder, aan haar voorbeeld en groot geloof zal hun levenslang een steun zijn in de moeilijkheden van het leven. Heer, wij bevelen U aan de ziel van Uw trouwe dienares, opdat zij, voor de wereld gestorven, voor U leve; wat zij door de zwakheid van het menselijk leven heeft misdreven, wis dat uit door de kwijtschelding van Uw barmhartigste liefde. Door Christus, onzen Heer. Amen.

„DE IJSELSTROOM" ULFT

Note: In this period the focus was on providing prayers for the deceased.

Source: From the family archive of Claudia Venhorst (the deceased is her great-grandmother).

Image 6.6. Typical Modern Mourning Card 2014.

Ter herinnering aan

Henri Jozef Venhorst

Geboren op 5 november 1919 te Gendringen
Overleden op 25 maart 2014 te Reuver

50 jaar in de echt verbonden geweest met

Dina Kiltaars †

Het is dinsdagmiddag 25 maart.
Buiten schijnt de voorjaarszon. Tijdens de prachtige klanken van
Albinoni's Adagio glijdt Pa zacht uit het leven.
Wij zitten bij hem en zullen dit moment nooit meer vergeten...

Wij danken U voor Uw steun en aanwezigheid tijdens dit afscheid.
Speciaal dank aan dokter Mensing en Harry Hillekens en zijn team in
Bosdael, voor de liefdevolle verzorging van Pa in de laatste periode
van zijn leven.

Met veel verdriet en respect nemen wij afscheid
van onze Pa, Opa en Opa-Henri

Nooit zou hij klagen, dat lag niet in zijn aard.
Hij wilde niemand tot last zijn en zocht liever zelf zijn grenzen op.
Had altijd een luisterend oor voor wie met zijn problemen bij hem aanklopte.
Hij geloofde in een goed gesprek bij het oplossen van conflicten en niet in de confrontatie. Hij bleef beschaafd onder alle omstandigheden. Hij was loyaal aan wie hem het vertrouwen schonk. Integer, bescheiden en nooit zelfzuchtig.
Hij was ruimdenkend, had zijn eigen mening, maar respecteerde ook die van een ander. "Leven en laten leven", zei hij dan.
Was oprecht geïnteresseerd in de mens, de politiek, maar vooral in het wel en wee in zijn familie.
Hij genoot van de mooie dingen die hij in zijn lange leven meemaakte: muziek, de natuur, rozen en de reizen naar andere culturen.
Die deelde hij ook graag met anderen en kon er enthousiast over vertellen.
Zo was hij.....

Een lieve vader en aimabel mens is heen gegaan.
Wij zijn hem heel dankbaar voor al het goede dat hij ons heeft meegegeven en waarmee wij verder kunnen.
Wij zullen hem zeer missen.

Source: From the family archive of Claudia Venhorst (the deceased is her grandfather).
Note: The card provides a very personal in memoriam of the deceased, including a picture on the cover. The deceased is the son of Wilhelmina Venhorst-Klein.

6.7.11. After the Funeral Service

After the funeral service, the funeral participants typically offer their condolences to the immediate family. This is often combined with or followed by a social gathering, the aforementioned coffee-table. This event may last from 45 minutes to a few hours; in some regions, communities and families it may continue for days. The funeral participants may also visit the graves or memorials of other deceased kith and kin, if they exist at the grounds of the funeral location.

CHAPTER 7

BURIAL AND CEMETERIES

7.1. HISTORIC DEVELOPMENT

For centuries burial was the preferred and only form of bodily disposal of the dead in the Netherlands. From the Middle Ages the (Roman Catholic) Church facilitated burial rites, providing burial space in its churches, chapels and churchyards. In the eighteenth century, when elsewhere in Europe burials in churches and cities were banned due to health concerns and lack of space, the Dutch tenaciously continued the practice despite all of its problems. It was, for instance, difficult to frequently break open the church floor, and according to a Dutch folk tale this resulted a lingering odour of corpses within the building.[1]

In the eighteenth and nineteenth centuries the dead were increasingly seen as a source of disease and as a danger to the living. Yet, people were also concerned about the dignity of

[1]Though factually incorrect, the Dutch expression *stinkend rijk* 'stinking rich' is often related to these burials. Retrieved from http://www.meertens.knaw.nl/cms/nl/nieuws-agenda/nieuwsbrief/vraag-van-de-maand/145021-vraag-van-mei-2016-rijke-stinkerd

the dead. Therefore, new cemeteries began to be constructed outside of places of settlement. In the 1869 Burial Act, the government successfully enforced the legal ban on church burials, and effectively put them to an end. The Act prescribed that no cemetery was to be built within 50 metres of a municipality's built-up area, and it was no longer allowed to access or enter a grave or vault in churches or other closed buildings.

The type of cemeteries that we know in the Netherlands today emerged in the late eighteenth century. They were purposely established on the outskirts of populated areas, and their spacious and park-like character became increasingly popular from the nineteenth century onwards. The first cemetery of this kind was set up in an isolated dune area outside Scheveningen in 1779 and was named *Ter Navolging* – To be Followed – to emphasise its exemplary role. The cemetery was founded by Abraham Perrenot, a Swiss born lawyer and politician. He studied law in Utrecht and obtained a doctorate in 1748 on the thesis 'On the prohibition of burial in the city and churches'.[2] The cemetery has no upright headstones and strongly resembles a church floor. Its typical style received no follow-up, despite its encouraging name. Nowadays 'Ter Navolging' is surrounded by buildings, and the privately owned cemetery is still in use.[3]

After the Second World War, cemetery provisions became increasingly minimalistic. A more efficient approach was taken towards burial grounds. Although cemeteries generally remained green havens, particularly in urban areas, the idyllic landscaping of the Romantic era adapted to a more practical use of space, making maintenance much easier and more cost

---

[2]Van Raak, C. (1995). *Dodenakkers*. Amsterdam: Arbeiderspers, 215–216.
[3]Retrieved from https://ternavolging.nl/. Accessed on April 3, 2019.

effective. Austerity was also promoted through rather elaborate local cemetery regulations and through a very limited choice of grave coverings – one could often choose from two types of (rather similar) headstones. As a result, cemeteries developed a quite uniform and controlled appearance from the 1950s throughout the 1980s. This development coincided with a further retrieval of death from public life.

The introduction of cremation as an alternative form of bodily disposal of the dead in the late nineteenth century initially met rather fierce opposition. Cremations sporadically took place from 1914 onwards, but were only officially legalised in the Corpse Disposal Act of 1955. In 2003, the number of cremations exceeded the number of burials for the first time, forcing cemetery managers and policymakers to re-evaluate cemetery provision and the burial business. As cemetery policies were initially directed towards the prevention of overcrowding, recently the number of burials has decreased so much that it threatens the viability of cemeteries.

7.2. CURRENT CEMETERY PROVISION

No clear number exists of operational burial sites in the Netherlands. The estimations vary between 3,500 and 4,000, but not all of these cemeteries are in use.[4] Most cemeteries offer space for full body interments as well as for ash disposal. About one-third of cemeteries in the Netherlands are municipal ones (*gemeentelijke begraafplaatsen*). Together, the municipal cemeteries provide 75% to 80% of all graves in

[4]Retrieved from https://www.dodenakkers.nl/naslag/statistieken/begraafplaatsstatistieken.html. Accessed on March 17, 2019.

the country.[5] The other cemeteries in the Netherlands are referred to as special cemeteries (*bijzondere begraafplaatsen*). They can be owned and operated by religious communities, foundations and private individuals.

To establish a special cemetery, one needs local authority approval, and the cemetery must correspond with other local development plans. Municipalities are encouraged – by national law and through governmental resources – to accommodate (religious) groups with appropriate burial options. They can allocate part of the municipal cemetery to a specific group, or support communities in creating a cemetery of their own. In recent years, natural burial grounds have become the most popular form of special cemeteries.

Finding suitable and affordable burial land can be a challenge in the Netherlands. Burial space is especially scarce in the western Randstad area, due to the dense population and the high levels of groundwater. Here, burials can only take place when a drainage system and an extra layer of earth are added.[6] In other areas, such as the Northeast, the type of soil (clay, peat) significantly slows down the process of decomposition. Only after substantial and often costly changes, such as adding great amounts of earth, the soil becomes burial-ready.[7]

The characteristics of the Dutch soil and the lack of space have led to a customary policy of clearing graves after a set

---

[5]van Dijk, S. & Mennen, M.G. (2002). *Lijkbezorging in Nederland. Evaluatie Inspectierichtlijn, Overzicht van de Branche en Inzicht in Naleving van Regelgeving*. Bilthoven: RIVM.

[6]Retrieved from https://www.begraafplaats.nl/de-begraafplaats/artikel/laat-u-de-kist-nog-in-de-prut-zakken/. Accessed on March 17, 2019.

[7]An overview of Dutch soil characteristics is given in Rijkswaterstaat (2014). *Into Dutch Soils*. Retrieved from https://rwsenvironment.eu/publish/pages/126603/into_dutch_soils.pdf

term. This term is generally set at 20 years, but it varies across the country. The Corpse Disposal Act prescribes a minimum burial period of 10 years, but does not refer to the practices of clearing graves. Although the number of deaths in the Netherlands is increasing, the firm policy of clearing graves and the decreasing number of burials – due to the rise of cremation – have caused a 'lack of occupancy' in many cemeteries.

Modern Dutch cemeteries have come into existence since the late nineteenth century (after the introduction of the first Burial Act in 1869) and from those early days on, facilitating diversity was a key aspect in municipal cemetery policies. Therefore, it is difficult to give an unambiguous picture of the typical Dutch cemetery. Moreover, the practice of grave clearing after 20 years makes it difficult to see what a cemetery looked like in a certain period. The uniform look of the 1950s to the 1980s, for instance, with rows of similar grave coverings, has often been completely wiped out. One can discover individual headstones from that period but the adjoining gravestones have been cleared, and new burials with new types of grave coverings have taken place, breaking the uniformity. Cemeteries are generally separated from their surroundings by walls, fences or hedges and accessible through a gate.

7.2.1. Municipal Cemeteries

By law, each municipality must attain at least one local burial site for all of its residents. The municipality thus owns and manages a cemetery that is available to all. Burials cannot be refused, and they make an effort to accommodate the burial needs and wishes of their local population. In the cemetery management regulations (*model-beheersverordening begraafplaatsen*) of the Association of

Dutch Municipalities – *Vereniging Nederlandse Gemeenten* (VNG) – it is explained as follows:[8]

> *Citizens often have an emotional involvement with cemeteries and everything that goes on there [...] The responsibility of the municipality for a cemetery can be compared to the responsibility it has for the care of other collective facilities such as walking areas and cycle paths. The different aspects of the cemeteries require a special approach from an administrative point of view. It is therefore proposed to involve experts in municipal cemeteries by setting up an advisory committee (in accordance with Article 84 of the Municipalities Act) that can advise the Municipal Executive on the general aspects of the cemetery and on the implementation of decisions. This includes experts in the field of mourning, local history and monuments. But also holders of grave rights and local residents [...] The municipality provides an extensive range of facilities for cemetery services [...] This regulation stipulates that the municipality is, in principle, prepared to take necessary measures. That does not mean that all facilities must actually be present at every municipal cemetery. It may be advisable to wait until demand arises before making certain factual provisions. It is important to record and announce*

[8]The VNG organisation represents the interests of all Dutch municipalities towards the central government, it delivers services for municipalities and offers its members a platform. VGN accommodates the constant improvement of municipal cemetery policies and provides cemetery management regulations.

> *that the municipality is, in principle, prepared to offer these facilities as soon as it appears that there is a need.*[9]

Already in the early twentieth century, the municipal cemetery reflected the wishes of diverse groups in society. Burial space was provided for different pillars, though their burial plots were strictly separated by walls and hedges. These boundaries continue to exist in a subtler form today, for instance in distinct Roman Catholic or Muslim burial areas. Although the cemetery as a whole is owned by the municipality, certain parts or plots can be owned and/or managed by other, often religious, institutions. The parts that are made available to church communities fall under the management of the municipality and the general regulations, although some specific additional rules might be in place. The municipal cemetery administration is responsible for the smooth running of daily affairs and also provides minimal maintenance of the grave coverings.[10]

The cemetery premises may host various practical buildings, such as the home of the cemetery manager and/or an office (with restrooms and a kitchenette), storage space, historical buildings like small morgues (*lijkenhuisje*) and tiny chapels (in Roman Catholic areas). Larger multipurpose buildings that could host farewell ceremonies exist, but are not common. They are often provided by funeral homes or commercial parties, and not necessarily situated at or near burial grounds. Alternatively, an open space might be used for services at the cemetery.

---

[9]VNG (2010). *Toelichting model-beheersverordening begraafplaatsen.* Retrieved from https://vng.nl/files/vng/20100203_ledenbrief_vng_10_015_model_beheersverordening_begraafplaasten.pdf

[10]VNG (2010).

7.2.2. Special Cemeteries

Special cemeteries cover a wide variety of cemeteries. The vast majority of these burial grounds are initiated and administered by religious institutions, such as the Roman Catholic or Reformed Church. Alternatively, they might have been developed by a foundation or individual in view of a certain idea or ideal, such as offering a natural burial ground or preserving a historic cemetery. Under strict conditions, it is also possible to establish a family cemetery on private land. However, this is not common practice (Image 7.1).

7.2.2.1. Roman Catholic

Roman Catholic cemeteries in the Netherlands emerged as classic graveyards, with graves in (close proximity of) local

Image 7.1. Grave Candle Vending Machine at Rustoord Cemetery in Nijmegen, Gelderland.

Note: Rustoord cemetery is special burial ground owned by Funeral Company Monuta.

Source: Photograph by Claudia Venhorst, 2015.

parish churches. In the Roman Catholic tradition, there has always been a strong connection between theology, the faith community and the cemetery. For Roman Catholics today it is no longer essential to bury near a church or chapel.[11] The cemetery typically is a site of consecrated ground where the deceased are buried according to the Catholic rites. A Calvary (a small hill with a crucifix on top, in a wide variety of sizes) or a Lourdes Grotto might take a central place at the cemetery when there is no church or chapel nearby.

Roman Catholic burial plots are often situated at the municipal cemetery, where certain facilities, such as the maintenance of plants, trees and lanes, can be shared with other cemetery users. The designated plots continue to be leased and managed by local parishes.[12] In 2003 the brochure 'Resting in Consecrated Ground' was published, offering practical guidelines for administrators of Roman Catholic cemeteries.[13] To a large extent the brochure discusses the challenge of shaping and maintaining a Roman Catholic identity in the contemporary Netherlands, where an increasing number of people have loosened ties with the church. The cemetery provides space for expressing Roman Catholic identity through symbolism. The image of Christ on the cross, mediating angels and saints who emphasise the relationship between the living and the dead, and the inclusion of a chapel on the premises are highly encouraged (Image 7.2). The practical implementation is laid down in 'a model cemetery

[11]R.K. Kerkgenootschap (2013). *Rusten in gewijde aarde. Katholieke begraafplaats en identiteit. Handreiking voor beheerders van katholieke begraafplaatsen*. Retrieved from https://www.begraafplaats.nl/de-begraafplaats/artikel/rusten-in-gewijde-aarde/
[12]R.K. Kerkgenootschap (2013).
[13]R.K. Kerkgenootschap (2013).

Image 7.2. Roman Catholic Cemetery in Nijmegen, Gelderland.

Note: Early twentieth-century grave monument, an elegantly decorated cross on a family grave.

Source: Photograph by Claudia Venhorst, 2017.

regulation for a Roman Catholic Parish of the Dutch Roman Catholic Church province'.[14]

The importance of the cemetery in the Roman Catholic tradition and its potential in maintaining Catholic identity was re-emphasised in October 2016, when the Congregation for the Doctrine of the Faith prohibited the disposal of cremated remains in non-sacred places, such as in the domestic sphere. According to the Vatican Instruction, 'burial in a cemetery or another sacred place adequately corresponds to the piety and respect owed to the bodies of the faithful departed who through Baptism have become temples of the Holy Spirit …'[15].

7.2.2.2. Protestant

With the introduction of the five *Solae* of the Protestant Reformation – a set of principles indicating that salvation could not be obtained through human action, but only by the grace of God – the common practice of praying for the salvation of the deceased was critiqued and eventually abolished in Protestant churches. This would have a significant impact on the role of the cemetery within the Protestant community. Grave visits were considered undesirable and continuing bonds with the dead were discouraged, although the large number of statements of the Synod of the Dutch Reformed

[14]R.K. Kerkgenootschap (2010). *Modelreglement voor het beheer van een begraafplaats van een R.-K. parochie van de Nederlandse R.-K. Kerkprovincie*. Retrieved from https://www.rkkerk.nl/wp-content/uploads/2018/02/15.-Modelreglement-R.-K-Begraafplaatsen.pdf

[15]Congregation for the Doctrine of the Faith (2016). *Instruction Ad resurgendum cum Christo regarding the burial of the deceased and the conservation of the ashes in the case of cremation*. The Holy See Press Office. Retrieved from http://www.vatican.va/roman_curia/congregations/cfaith/documents/rc_con_cfaith_doc_20160815_ad-resurgendum-cum-christo_en.html. Accessed on May 12, 2019.

Church on this matter reflect the difficulty of maintaining this ideal (for both ministers and the bereaved).[16]

When cemeteries were established at the outskirts of towns in the late eighteenth and nineteenth century, and when the Reformed Churches expressed the necessity of church involvement in burials in 1905, Protestants opted for their own 'designated' cemeteries near local churches.[17] Municipal cemeteries also allocated specific burial sections for Protestants or for specific denominations. Today these designated plots are owned and managed by the various protestant churches. Practical and legal issues are addressed in the model regulations for the management of Protestant (PKN) cemeteries.[18]

Protestant cemeteries are characterised by a distinct material culture, shaped by their theology that critiqued Roman Catholic practice. Emphasising a stark boundary between life and death, Protestants used symbols that expressed the finitude of life: open bibles, extinguished torches, cracked jugs, empty hourglasses, urns, laurel wreaths and truncated columns. Most characteristic is the overwhelming use of biblical quotes and references on headstones (Image 7.3). The varieties of objects and flowers that can be observed at some contemporary Protestant graves, especially of those who belong to moderate faith communities, reveal changing and increasingly personal burial and grave visiting customs.

---

[16]Van den Broeke, L. (2015). 'No funeral sermons: Dutch or Calvinistic prohibition?'. In T. Rasmussen & J. Øygarden Flæten (eds.). *Preparing for Death, Remembering the Dead.* Göttingen: Vandenhoeck & Ruprecht, 361–377.

[17]Boon, R. (1987). 'De 'laatste eer' in gereformeerd-protestants milieu. Een geschiedenis van verwerping en eerherstel.' *Eredienstvaardig*, 3 (5).

[18]Vereniging voor Kerkrentmeesterlijk Beheer in de Protestantse Kerk in Nederland (2016). *Model-reglement voor het beheer van de begraafplaats van de Protestantse gemeente.* Retrieved from https://admin.begraafplaats.nl/media/654.pdf

Image 7.3. The Old Cemetery in Sauwerd, Groningen, with Protestant Headstones.

Source: Photograph by Brenda Mathijssen, 2018.

7.2.2.3. Jewish

Jewish cemeteries are among the oldest in the Netherlands, as the Jewish communities were the first to establish separate burial sites. The oldest Jewish cemetery in the Netherlands is Beth Haim, in Ouderkerk aan de Amstel, established in 1614. Congregations had settled all over the country, in both cities and towns. However, due to the Holocaust, the number of Jews in the Netherlands has diminished severely. Today over 200 Jewish cemeteries exist, but most of them are no longer serving a living local community. Cemeteries are held in high regard in Jewish traditions. They have the same sanctity as a synagogue and those who visit the cemetery grounds should behave accordingly. According to the Jewish faith, cemeteries belong to those who are buried there, to those who have found their final resting place at them. They cannot be closed and the graves cannot be cleared. Therefore, the cemeteries of former congregations continue to exist. They function as silent witnesses of the Jewish life and lives that disappeared from particular areas (Image 7.4). Occasionally, Jewish descendants who now live elsewhere choose to be buried at the old cemetery of their former home town. Jewish cemeteries in the Netherlands are generally private property. They are cared for by the Organisation of Jewish Communities in the Netherlands (the NIK) in cooperation with the local municipalities.[19]

7.2.2.4. Muslim

Since the 1990s, many municipal cemeteries in the Netherlands have allocated designated Muslim burial areas. These Islamic sections accommodate the various wishes and requirements of the diverse Muslim community, such as only one burial per grave, being buried in the direction of Mecca, being buried in a chamber, and having a modest grave design (Image 7.5). The absence of eternal graves is a challenge for many Muslims in the Netherlands. Extended grave rights are often offered, typically for 40 years instead of the regular 20, but eternal graves cannot be guaranteed. Grave rights can always be extended, but this is a rather costly affair that is not affordable for all.

Today only one special independent Islamic cemetery exists in the Netherlands. The cemetery is owned by the mosque organisation Ar-Raza in Almere and offers the promise of perpetuity. A complete adult funeral, including a grave

[19]For more information about the NIK, see http://www.nik.nl/de-zorg-voor-de-joodse-begraafplaatsen/. Accessed on March 17, 2019.

Image 7.4. Jewish Cemetery in Dwingeloo, Drenthe.

Notes: The cemetery opened in 1830, but the local Jewish community was dismantled in 1950. The cemetery is currently maintained by the local authority, and photographs of the tomb stones have been stored in the Archive of Stone.[20]
Source: Photograph by Brenda Mathijssen, 2017.

at the cemetery, costs approximately €8,500. Those who regularly donate to the mosque receive a discount on the funeral fees. Muslims from across the country are buried in this cemetery, and there are plans to establish another independent Islamic burial site.

7.2.2.5. Natural Burial Grounds

Natural Burial grounds are a relatively new and increasingly popular phenomenon in the Netherlands. The first natural burial ground opened in 1944 at the Westerwolde estate in Assel,

[20]Retrieved from https://www.stenenarchief.nl/. Accessed on March 17, 2019.

Image 7.5. Muslim Burial Site, Grave Plots at Municipal Cemetery Blerickse Bergen in Venlo, Limburg.

Note: Burials have been taking place here since 1995.
Source: Photograph by Claudia Venhorst, 2016.

but natural burial only became a trend in the early twenty-first century. Currently 18 burial grounds exist, most of which have been developed as private (commercial) initiatives. They are mainly situated in existing wood-, heath- and meadowlands in the eastern part of the Netherlands where the soil and water levels are suitable, and where construction is profitable. Plans exist to further develop natural burial sites, for instance in land owned by the national natural conservation organisation Natuurmonumenten Nederland. In this case the creation of a natural burial site at a so-called Natural Monument, a valuable natural area or landscape, is meant to generate funds for further development or preservation of those sites.[21]

[21]Retrieved from https://www.natuurmonumenten.nl/natuurbegraven. Accessed on April 9, 2019.

Although many cemeteries in the Netherlands are situated in natural areas or are designed as green parks or garden landscapes, a small but increasing number of people are choosing natural burial. According to BRANA, the trade association for natural burial in the Netherlands, natural burials have increased from 10 in 2011 to 617 in 2016, with burials accounting for 0.4% of all deaths.[22] The choice for natural burial is not simply a matter of location in the Netherlands. People appreciate the romantic idea of returning to nature, and the symbolism of the natural cycle of life and death. These are strongly linked to natural burial and used as a marketing tool. Also, the freedom of choosing a specific burial plot is appealing to many. Furthermore, ecological motives play a role. Whereas some argue that natural burial guarantees the continued existence of specific areas as nature reserves, nature organisations and local residents have also been critical. Although the practice is not harmful to the composition of the soil, root systems can be seriously affected if too many funerals take place. In addition, trees and plants often have to be removed to make the soil ready for burial. People also opt for a final resting place in the forest for practical reasons. Costly grave markers or headstones are not allowed and the graves do not have to be kept. Therefore, the next of kin do not face 'the burden' of grave maintenance.[23] Moreover, burial is granted in perpetuity so the grave does not need to be cleared.

The regulations on grave coverings generally are very strict at natural burial sites. Usually only native plants or natural

[22]Retrieved from http://brana.nu/wat-is-natuurbegraven/feiten-en-cijfers-over-natuurbegraven-in-nederland/. Accessed April 9, 2019.

[23]This perceived burden is one of people's main motives to choose for cremation. See Mathijssen (2017a) and (2017b). 'The ambiguity of human ashes: Exploring encounters with cremated remains in the Netherlands'. *Death Studies*. 41 (1), 34–41.

materials are permitted as grave decorations. However, these regulations are much ignored. Observations show that people appear to have a strong inclination to mark and personalise a grave with objects like flowers, bird houses, children's drawings and photographs.[24] Although such decorations violate the regulations and principles of natural burial, many natural burial ground keepers struggle with the enforcement as it means that they actively have to remove those grave goods. This is generally not taken well by the next of kin who regularly visit the grave.

Natural burial is not mentioned as a specific type of burial in the 1991 Corpse Disposal Act. According to some lobbying organisations, this leads to confusion about the legal status of natural burial. When a proposal was made to renew legislation in November 2018 it was suggested to incorporate natural burial grounds in the law to clarify that these sites uphold to the general cemetery regulations (Images 7.6 and 7.7).[25]

7.2.2.6. War Cemeteries

War cemeteries in the Netherlands are few. Due to the neutral status of the Netherlands, the Dutch military forces did not participate in the First World War. At the cemeteries of the Second World War, foreign soldiers have predominantly been laid to rest (Image 7.8). These include those that were killed while liberating the country (mainly British, Canadian and American) as well as those that were killed while occupying it (Germans). The Grebbeberg Military Cemetery is the last resting place of over 400 Dutch soldiers who fell in May 1940. The Loenen Field of Honour was founded in 1947 to accommodate a wide

---

[24]Venhorst, C. & Mathijssen, B. (2017). *Dood. Wegwijs in de Nederlandse Uitvaartcultuur*. Almere: Parthenon, 69.

[25]D66 (2018). Initiatiefnota Moderne Uitvaartwet. Retrieved from https://d66.nl/content/uploads/sites/2/2018/11/Initiatiefnota-Moderne-Uitvaartwet.pdf

Image 7.6. Grave at a Natural Burial Ground in Blerick/ Maasbree, Limburg.

Source: Photograph by Claudia Venhorst, 2016.

variety of victims: fallen soldiers and many civilians like resistance fighters, political prisoners and victims of forced employment (*Arbeitseinsatz*) in Germany (see also 9.2).

7.2.2.7. Pet Cemeteries

Across the country, about 50 pet cemeteries and crematoria can be found that provide funerary services for people's

Image 7.7. Open Air Auditorium at Natural Burial Ground in Blerick/Maasbree, Limburg.

Source: Photograph by Claudia Venhorst, 2016.

Image 7.8. Canadian War Cemetery and Memorial in Groesbeek, Gelderland.

Note: At this Second World War military cemetery, 2,619 burials have taken place.
Source: Photograph by Claudia Venhorst taken during the annual candle lighting commemoration on Christmas Eve 2016.

Image 7.9. 'You are the sweetest dog'. A Memorial Plaque at the Pet Cemetery in Grashoek, Limburg.

Source: Photograph by Claudia Venhorst, 2016.
Note: This is the first natural burial ground for pets in the Netherlands.

domestic animals. Pets are increasingly treated like full-fledged family members and pet burial and memorial trends develop much in line with human funerals. In the town of Grashoek in the northern part of Limburg, the first natural burial ground for small pets was opened. Pets from all over the country are buried here (Image 7.9) or had their ashes scattered. The facility also holds a national memorial for missing domestic animals and a memorial site for the dogs that died aboard flight MH17 in 2014.

7.3. GRAVES

The 1991 Corpse Disposal Act mentions two types of graves: general and private. A general grave is leased by the next of kin, and controlled and maintained by the cemetery manager.

The cemetery administration determines who is buried in which grave and for what period. A general grave can thus accommodate several deceased who are unrelated or unacquainted, and there typically are several memorials covering the burial plot. The anonymous dead are also buried in this type of grave. After the minimum grave term of 10 years – or 15 or 20 years, depending on the local regulations – the grave is cleared. There is no option for renewal. General graves, often the most affordable option, are typically offered in crowded cemeteries that are rather expensive, and are not available in every cemetery.

In the case of a private grave, one obtains the rights to a burial site – the so-called grave rights or *grafrechten*. With the purchase one becomes the rightful claimant according to the law. The owner of the cemetery remains the owner of the land, but the person holding the grave rights can largely determine what happens to the grave. S/he for instance decides who will be buried in this grave and for how long it will remain. Although the rightful claimant has obtained the grave rights and therefore decides about what grave monument will be placed, the latter has to comply to the local cemetery regulations (in which the rules of the national Corpse Disposal Act are conveyed). With acquiring 'grave rights' one also takes on some (financial) duties concerning maintenance and safety issues.

7.3.1. Technicalities

The additional order to the Corpse Disposal Act, the *Besluit op de Lijkbezorging*, regulates the layout of new graves.[26] The order prescribes that the distance between graves must at

[26]Retrieved from https://wetten.overheid.nl/BWBR0009080/2013-01-01, Artikel 5.

Image 7.10. Overview of a Burial Plot at Municipal Cemetery Venlo, Limburg, with New Graves.

Source: Photograph by Claudia Venhorst, 2016.

least be 30 centimetres (Image 7.10). The layer of soil on top of the coffin or casing should at least be 65 cm. No more than three corpses may be buried on top of each other, provided that a layer of soil of at least 30 cm is applied on top of each coffin or other covering. This layer may not be disturbed at a subsequent burial, and the layer of soil on top of the latest coffin or covering must be 65 cm. The graves are at least 30 cm above the highest average groundwater level.

The graves at old cemeteries are 80 × 200 cm. Because the average height of people has increased over the last 100 years, and because modern digging equipment requires more space, the old grave size has become too tight. Today a grave width of 100 cm, preferably even 120 cm, is used when enough burial space exists at the cemetery. The length of the grave is typically 220 or 250 cm. It is customary to use a smaller monument or headstone on top of the grave, for instance of 100 × 200 cm.[27] Cemeteries typically offer a variety of graves with different appearances to accommodate the diverse burial wishes of people: the common sand graves, a bricked tomb or vaulted grave, 'above-ground graves' or columbaria, niches, or other edifices.[28] Urn graves, a columbarium or urn wall, and an ash scattering facility are also generally available.

The Corpse Disposal Act does not mention grave coverings, this topic is generally addressed in the local cemetery regulations. 'Grave covering' commonly refers to a grave monument as well as permanent (hardy) planting on graves. The model regulations for municipal cemeteries stresses the need for such regulations, as without them the cemetery appearance can become chaotic and the safety of visitors might be at risk.[29] In the same document cemetery managers are also advised to provide citizens the necessary freedom and limit regulations to minimum requirements for the dimensions, construction and choice of durable materials. A grave monument is not obligatory but it should be indicated that someone is buried there to prevent visitors from accidentally walking over the grave. There is also an indication needed for administrative purposes. Special burial grounds commonly provide more specified regulations for grave coverings.

---

[27]Retrieved from https://www.uitvaart.nl/juridisch/begraven/aanleggen-begraafplaats-e-d/voorwaarden-van-de-grond-om-er-een-begraafplaats-van-te-maken/49831. Accessed March 12, 2019.

[28]Information on sand soil can be found in Rijkswaterstaat (2014). *Into Dutch soils*. Retrieved from https://rwsenvironment.eu/publish/pages/126603/into_dutch_soils.pdf.

[29]VNG (2010). *Toelichting model-beheersverordening begraafplaatsen*. Retrieved from https://vng.nl/files/vng/20100203_ledenbrief_vng_10_015_model_beheersverordening_begraafplaasten.pdf

7.3.2. Grave Rights and Terms

The grave rights to a private grave are issued for a minimum period of 10 years – the legal minimum – although 20 years is more common. Some cemeteries offer extended terms of 30 to 50 years. The law does allow grave rights to be issued indefinitely. However, this seldom is an option as the costs are (too) high. Most cemetery administrators do not see it as a feasible option, so eternal grave rights are simply not offered when there is no need to do so – like for example for religious reasons.

At least one year before the grave rights expire, the rightful claimant will receive a letter from the cemetery management with an offer to extend the grave rights for another period of five or 10 years at a special renewal fee. The possibility of extension must be offered at the end of each term.[30] This guarantees that private graves can be kept as long as the rights are renewed and paid for, and the maintenance obligation is met. This care/maintenance obligation is part of the lease agreement, meaning the owner is responsible for the safety of monuments or coverings placed on the grave. Generally, there is also an obligatory maintenance fee, which applies to overall maintenance of the cemetery grounds and an annual cleaning of the gravesite – regulations, definitions of maintenance and costs can vary between cemeteries.

Acquired grave rights of a private grave cannot be sold, but they can be – upon request of the current owner – transferred to another individual or legal person. In case of the death of the owner, a request for transferral must be made within six months after this. If the rightful claimant does not renew the grave rights, they expire and go back to the

[30]Retrieved from https://www.begraafplaats.nl/wat-is-grafrecht/. Accessed on March 12, 2019.

cemetery administrator. The administrator subsequently decides how and when the grave will be cleared.[31]

7.3.3. Clearing of Graves

Although not arranged by law, Dutch cemeteries have a policy of clearing graves when the grave rights are not renewed and expire. The first step is to remove the visible grave coverings, like the headstone or the cover plate (see Section 7.3.5) (Image 7.11). The human remains could be left untouched for quite some time. General graves are often directly cleared in their entirety to make room for new burials. The excavated remains are then collectively reburied in a closed off area at the cemetery. Private graves are often only cleared when a new burial takes place. At the day of the new burial the grave will be further excavated, and the remains moved to a lower level in the grave. After adding a layer of earth, a new burial can take place.

After 10 years of grave rest, the holder of the grave rights can request an exhumation to rebury the deceased elsewhere or to cremate the remains. Cemetery and municipal regulations prohibit people – other than the professionals doing their work – to be present when clearing out graves. The clearing is generally done by specialised companies, and the area has to be shielded off from the public.[32]

---

[31]VGN (2010).

[32]In order to protect employees from the possible emotional reactions of the bereaved when present, as demanded by the Working Conditions Legislation (*Arbowet*), municipal and cemetery regulations order that clearings as well as exhumations should be done by professionals only in a shielded off area. More information is available in publications of the National burial grounds Association or Landelijke Organisatie van Begraafplaatsen (LOB). LOB (2018). *Handboek Opgraven en Ruimen*. Amsterdam; LOB (2017). *Veilig en gezond werken op begraafplaatsen, Arbo-richtlijnen in de praktijk* (2007, updated in 2015). Amsterdam.

Image 7.11. Open Spaces at the Cemetery after Grave Plot Clearance.

Source: Photograph by Claudia Venhorst, taken at the Municipal cemetery Venlo, Limburg, 2016.

Note: When grave plots are partially cleared out, open spaces arise.

7.3.4. Burial Costs

Grave costs vary greatly per province and even per municipality. Annual research by Monuta, examining 1,679 cemeteries in 379 municipalities, shows that burial costs can be two times higher in the Randstad than in the south of the country.[33] The average cost of a single grave in 2018 was €2,812, with €7,129 the most expensive grave found at the municipal cemetery Esserveld in Groningen (Image 7.12). The least expensive graves are available for €721 at the municipal cemetery Bookholtlaan in Losser, Overijssel. On

[33]Retrieved from https://www.monuta.nl/grafkostenmeter/. Accessed on March 14, 2019.

Image 7.12. Esserveld Cemetery, Groningen: The Most Expensive Cemetery in the Netherlands.

Source: Photograph by Brenda Mathijssen, 2018.

average, private graves are the most affordable in the province of Limburg (€1,833), whereas the average cost for the same grave amounts to € 3,494 in North-Holland.[34]

A number of factors contribute to the differences in burial costs. First, the price of land impacts the burial costs. In the Randstad the average price of land is high, which leads to an increased burial expense. Second, the required maintenance at the cemetery may result in higher or lower costs. Cemeteries, for instance, may be smaller or larger, with special landscaping or architectural features, and can have a central or more remote location. Third, supply and demand will

[34]Retrieved from https://www.monuta.nl/over-monuta/nieuws/grote-verschillen-gemeentelijke-grafkosten-2018/. Accessed on April 14, 2019.

impact the burial fees: the decrease of burials and the rise of cremation play a role. Fourth, the choice between a private or a general grave influences the price. Fifth, staffing and cemetery management influence the burial expense. Church-owned cemeteries are generally cheaper because volunteers take care of maintenance, and because members have already financially contributed throughout the years. Graves on natural burial grounds can be attractive in terms of costs because they do not have to be maintained.

Burial costs and the cost for a grave monument are generally not covered by Dutch funeral insurances (see Section 5.3).

7.3.5. Grave Covers

In Dutch cemeteries a wide variety of grave covers can be observed, which vary in cost between €1,000 and €2,500.[35] Grave monuments are provided by a wide range of suppliers, both funeral directors and cemetery management can advise and offer guidance in the matter. Most suppliers are well represented online with direct information on possibilities and prices. In addition to standing and/or lying marble or natural stones or boulders, there are memorials of wood, glass, Perspex or metal.[36] One can opt for a unique design, for special lettering or a common symbol. The market – varying from traditional local stone masons to private artists – encourages and enables people to use personal designs and images. Garden centres supply suitable grave

[35]Warnaar, M., Stoof, R. & Schonewille, G. (2017). *Kennis en bewustzijn van uitvaartkosten*. Utrecht: Nibud. The report is retrieved from https://www.nibud.nl/wp-content/uploads/Nibud-rapport-Kennis-en-bewustzijn-van-uitvaartkosten.pdf

[36]Retrieved from https://www.uitvaart.nl/infotheek/het-graf/grafmonumenten-grafstenen-gedenktekens

planting, as well as semi-permanent decorations. The material, the symbolism and the text of the grave covering typically refer to the deceased. Moreover, the monument gives a statement of the bereaved. This rather personal approach is generally facilitated by cemetery regulations that permit optimal freedom of expression within a minimal setting of requirements concerning measurements, safety and durability of used materials. What might be considered a typical grave covering varies regionally and even locally.

Graves in the Netherlands are marked with the name(s) of the deceased, and the dates of birth and of death. By naming and dating a random piece of stone (or other durable material) it unmistakably becomes a gravestone, and the grave loses its anonymity. In case of a double or family grave, it is not uncommon to already include the name of the surviving spouse on the headstone. Epitaphs on grave coverings vary according to personal preferences, and socio-economic and cultural diversity. They may include wishes to the deceased, expressions of love and gratitude of the next of kin and references to religious scripture.

Although graves are often temporal, the durable monuments (in particular material like marble and granite) seem to be made for eternity. Therefore, cemeteries may give the impression that the dead continue to exist in a very literal sense. The marble may be a source of comfort to those visiting the cemetery. When graves are cleared, the covering inscribed with names and dates is removed. The monument is property of the owner of the grave but most people do not want to keep the grave monument, especially not when it is a 100 × 200 cm cover stone. Some of the grave stones are reused while others are processed into rubble, or are used elsewhere at the cemetery. Some cemeteries and organisations have started to archive (photographs of) cleared headstones.

In addition to the permanent coverings, graves are decorated by a variety of improvised and semi-permanent items: candles (LED or other), figurines, angels and butterflies, (plastic) flowers and plants, photos, cards and notes. These grave objects are often very common items, mass produced and sold at garden centres and chain stores, and materialise the bonds between the living and the dead. People bring flowers on Mother's Day, 'send' birthday cards or place Christmas decorations. The stories and lives of the living become visible in the grave objects. The deceased may be congratulated on his birthday, or a daughter may announce her pregnancy to her deceased mother by placing a print of an ultrasound, and later by sharing baby photos (Image 7.13).

Image 7.13. Balloon-decorated Grave to Celebrate the Deceased's Birthday.

Source: Photograph taken at the Municipal cemetery in Venlo, Limburg, by Claudia Venhorst, 2016.

7.3.6. Preservation

Cemetery management in the Netherlands has long been pragmatic, with little attention for the preservation of funerary heritage. According to the municipal cemetery regulations it is up to the local cemetery managers 'to keep a list of graves of historical significance or of which the grave cover has striking quality'.[37] Graves are deemed significant because of the person buried there, or because of the grave memorial. The memorial may have an outstanding design or a special material may be used. In the regulations, cast iron is mentioned as an example of a material that recalls an industry long gone. Increasingly, measures are taken so that graves are no longer thoughtlessly cleared. As the maintenance and repair of graves is costly, the cemetery administration can apply for an official status as a national monument (*rijksmonument*). This status can apply to individual graves, gates and buildings, as well as to cemeteries as a whole.[38] Since the 1990s many local historical societies have made an effort to preserve local cemeteries and graves, often with the help of independent foundations, like 'Terebinth', who offer support and knowledge in the preservation of funerary culture in the Netherlands.[39] In addition to material culture, the preservation of immaterial culture is increasingly receiving attention. The expertise centre on immaterial heritage (*Kenniscentrum Immaterieel Erfgoed*) has been implementing the UNESCO international cultural treaty, since it was signed by the

[37]VNG (2010).
[38]Retrieved from http://www.rijksmonumenten.nl/monumenten/begraafplaats/. Accessed on April 10, 2019.
[39]Retrieved from http://www.terebinth.nl/. Accessed on April 10, 2019.

Netherlands in 2012. They aim to make immaterial heritage visible and accessible, and the All Souls celebration, the 'week of the cemetery' and the adoption of war graves are all listed.[40] Other emerging preservation initiatives include the digitalisation of grave memorials and cemeteries,[41] publishing stories behind grave stones and historical cemeteries[42] or art projects such as *'Sluipweg, waarlangs de dood heeft weten te ontsnappen'* [Shortcut, along which death has managed to escape] in which over 200 grave stones – contributed by the next of kin after a grave was cleared – are used to create an eternal path around Fort Vijfhuizen.[43]

7.4. CEMETERY VARIATION IN THE NETHERLANDS

Cemeteries are a collection of entangled individual grave sites. Together, the graves tell stories about the living and about their burial customs, their religious and cultural communities, their relationships with the dead and their relationships to each other. They reveal changes over time. As the examples below indicate, cemeteries illustrate contrasting and changing funerary practices in the Netherlands.

---

[40]Retrieved from https://www.immaterieelerfgoed.nl/nl/allerzielen; https://www.immaterieelerfgoed.nl/nl/page/2091/begraven-en-begraven-worden; & https://www.immaterieelerfgoed.nl/nl/adoptiegravenmargraten. Accessed on April 10, 2019.

[41]Retrieved from https://www.stenenarchief.nl/; https://www.online-begraafplaatsen.nl/; https://www.collectiegelderland.nl/zoeken/?q=grafmonumenten. Accessed on April 10, 2019.

[42]Retrieved from https://www.dodenakkers.nl/. Accessed on April 10, 2019.

[43]Retrieved from http://dhaps.org/kunstwerken/sluipweg-waarlangs-de-dood-heeft-weten-te-ontsnappen/. Accessed on April 10, 2019.

7.4.1. Marken and Volendam: Protestant and Catholic Traditions

The municipal cemetery on the former island of Marken is located on a mound and surrounded by trees (Image 7.14). Through the gate you enter the shell-covered area where the dead have been buried since 1820. There is no splendour here. Burials are performed in a strict Calvinist tradition in which everyone is equal before God. The dead are buried anonymously in general graves, where up to three people can be laid to rest. The graves are covered with numbered black cast-iron poles, serving administrative purposes only.[44] There are no headstones, no dates and no names at the grave, and no speeches and flowers at the burial. The vast majority of the villagers choose this type of burial, and there is an explicit aim and policy to preserve the sober Protestant character of the cemetery. Only a small section exists with private graves with modest grave covers.

Across the water of the Ijsselmeer, just five kilometres away, the graveyard of (mainly Catholic) Volendam has a very different appearance (Image 7.15). When the Vincentius Church was built in 1862, a churchyard was added. Here too the graves were initially only marked with a number. Later these were replaced by wooden crosses, and then by stone crosses with a name plaque. Today the cemetery almost exclusively holds general graves. Due to the lack of space the graves are laid close to each other, side by side. Each gravesite has room for three burials, and is furnished with an equal number of headstones.

[44]The sober burial style not only finds its origins in the Calvinist tradition, but has also been shaped by the island's relationship with water. Although the cemetery is situated on a mound, it often flooded and the simple burial slots and markers made it easier to deal with this.

Image 7.14. Protestant Cemetery of Marken, Noord Holland.

Source: Photograph by Claudia Venhorst, 2015.

Image 7.15. Roman Catholic Cemetery of Volendam, Noord Holland.

Source: Photograph by Claudia Venhorst, 2015.

The stones are densely decorated: besides the full name of the deceased, and often also the nickname, a photo and a memorial text have been added. The cemetery is usually covered in flowers. Because the cemetery is located in the town centre, the possibilities for an extension are limited. Therefore, all graves are cleared after 14 years, with the exception of the children's graves at a separate plot.

The cemeteries of Marken and Volendam reveal something about the burial traditions of Protestants and Roman Catholics in the Netherlands, and the severe contrast between the two. Although the differences are stark, these cemeteries are also exceptional. Nowhere else in the country, the contrast between Protestant and Roman Catholic death ways is so obvious.

7.4.2. Roermond: The Old Cemetery

One of the oldest Dutch cemeteries can be found In Roermond. Due to a lack of space and health and safety issues, burial within the churches and within the city walls was already banned in Roermond in 1784. The cemetery was founded in 1785 and has four strictly separated areas: Roman Catholic, Dutch Reformed, an old Jewish part and a new Jewish part. Such a division is not unique in the Netherlands, but the separation is almost nowhere as explicit as it is here. High brick walls stand between the various sections, segregating the burial plots. Because the cemetery was closed to new burials in 1948, with the exception of the new Jewish part and annexes in existing family graves, the brick walls have remained untouched. Elsewhere in the country such walls and hedges disappeared in view of reorganisations and modernisations. In addition to the four formal areas, there is a distinct section on the Catholic part of the cemetery. Separated by a private hedge, it is called the 'lost cemetery'.

Officially, those who did not belong to any denomination were buried here. In practice, although some indeed were buried here for principle reasons, the area was mainly used to inter suicide victims and unidentified bodies recovered from the river Maas. There is also the (unmarked) grave of an NSB member, a highly placed collaborator with the German occupation during the Second World War.

The Roermond cemetery is especially famous for the 'grave with the hands' (Image 7.16). In 1842 the 22-year-old Roman Catholic Lady Josephine van Aefferden married Colonel van Gorkum who was 11 years her senior, not of nobility, and a Protestant. After a marriage of nearly 40 years, the colonel died in 1880 and was buried in the Dutch Reformed section of the cemetery. When his wife passed away eight years later, she was not buried in the family grave. Instead, she chose a grave directly on the opposite Catholic

Image 7.16. Grave with the Hands at the Old Cemetery in Roermond, Limburg.

Source: Photograph by Claudia Venhorst, 2016.

side of her husband's. Two hands reach each other across the metre-high brick wall, linking the two graves and prolonging the mixed Protestant-Catholic marriage beyond death.

After closure in 1948, the cemetery fell into disrepair. It was restored in the 1990s, and in 2001 the entire cemetery was listed as a national monument due to the large collection of notable tombs and monuments with typical neo-Gothic art and cast-iron crosses. The historic morgue, the episcopal burial vault, the chapel, and over 600 graves have all been restored and are accessible to the public. There are also many children's graves that are still being visited. Unlike the many older monuments, these graves are decorated with fresh flowers and plants, little angel statues, candles and sometimes an entirely new monument. Since 2010 the cemetery has been reopened to accommodate new burials.

7.4.3. Amsterdam: De Nieuwe Ooster

De Nieuwe Ooster is the largest cemetery of Amsterdam, and creates a green oasis of 33 hectares within the cityscape. It was established in 1894 when the old Oosterbegraafplaats, within 20 years of its opening, rapidly ran out of burial land. The cemetery was designed as a burial park by landscape architect Leonard Springer and was situated in a more spacious area. This new type of cemetery, designed as a park or garden landscape, became an ideal in the Romantic era and can be found throughout the Netherlands.

Although many well-known artists and notable people are buried at De Nieuwe Ooster, the cemetery characterises itself as the cemetery for all residents of Amsterdam. All ranks and classes, denominations, and ethnic and cultural backgrounds have been given a place, reflecting the city's egalitarian character. While it is common practice in many European capitals to create special burial grounds for national political, military and cultural heroes, in the Netherlands they are usually buried in regular graves and across the country.

When De Nieuwe Ooster first opened, the cemetery strongly reflected differences in socio-economic class. Like elsewhere in the Netherlands, the wealthy could purchase their own (family) grave with generously sized tombs, whereas the less fortunate could only afford smaller leased graves with simple coverings. After the Second World War a strong tendency towards austerity developed in cemeteries: uniform grave coverings were prescribed and there was limited scope for variation and personalisation. The result was a rather egalitarian-looking burial site. Today many graves of the pre- and post-war period have been cleared, especially those of the common citizens. The extravagant tombs and above-ground graves of the wealthy have been extended and have occasionally received monumental status. The image of Dutch funerary culture, as it is reflected at cemeteries today, is therefore skewed.

In the 1990s the applicable cemetery regulations were reinterpreted, and people wanted to decorate the grave of their deceased in a more personal fashion. De Nieuwe Ooster responded to this trend by catering to the diverse wishes and needs of the public. In 1994 the already existing auditorium on the cemetery grounds was extended to include a crematorium. The building's welcoming and reception areas were enlarged and modernised, and in 2000 the original organ, the monumental interior and the wall paintings by Albert Muis were renovated. The cemetery grounds were also redeveloped. Landscape architects Karres and Brands renovated and restored the existing burial sections, and designed new ones to provide the bereaved with different options to commemorate their deceased. The general graves were enlarged, and have been placed at prominent locations to underline the egalitarian character of the cemetery. Above-ground graves were constructed and a natural burial area was designed. Also, areas at the cemetery were allocated to various forms of ash disposal, which is reflected in the scattering fields, sections for urn graves, a monumental urn wall and a water pond. Moreover, an Islamic burial area, funeral pavilion and ritual cleansing facility were established in 2011, in collaboration with six local Muslim organisations.

Lastly, a funeral museum exists at the cemetery grounds of De Nieuwe Ooster. *Tot Zover* opened in 2007, and offers a general collection on funerary culture, changing exhibitions, a variety of events and a restaurant and café.

7.4.4. Beth Haim: Portuguese Jewish Cemetery

Sephardim started arriving, from Portugal and Spain, in Amsterdam in the sixteenth century. After building a Synagogue they were granted permission in 1614 to establish a cemetery for their community in the small town of Ouderkerk aan de Amstel, near Amsterdam. For almost four centuries, the community has been burying its members at Beth Haim ('House of Life'). In 1923, the cemetery neared full capacity.[45] Because Jewish law forbids the exhumation of the dead, an old part of Beth Haim was covered with earth to create more space. It was estimated that there would be enough burial space for another 40 years, but due to the Holocaust the community was nearly decimated. The cemetery now holds 28,000 graves and has sufficient space for the next 80 years. It has been preserved in its original state.

[45]Retrieved from https://www.bethhaim.nl/geschiedenis/. Accessed on March 19, 2019.

In the Golden Age, the seventeenth century in particular, many splendid and unique marble memorial stones were used (Image 7.17). The tombstones have inscriptions in Dutch, Portuguese and Hebrew, and are carved with elaborate figurative scenes and mystic symbols. The funeral ceremonies take place at the Rodeamentos House. It was built in 1705 and divides the old part of the cemetery with historic monumental tombstones from the section containing relatively new graves (image 7.18).

Since 2009, Beth Haim is also the unexpected host of an annual commemoration ceremony for the abolition of slavery in Suriname and the Antilles.[46] It is attended by a few hundred representatives of Afro Surinam, Antilles and Jewish communities, and local government officials. The ceremony is held at the grave of Servo Elieser, a servant – possibly slave – of African origin, part of the household of the prominent De Pina family.[47] When Elieser died in 1629 he was given a prominent place and an engraved stone at the Jewish cemetery, which is seen as an exceptional gesture. The gravestone was discovered by accident in 2002 and reads: 'S(epultura) do bom servo Elieser', 'The grave of the good servant Elieser'.[48] Right outside the cemetery a statue of Elieser is placed and the adjoining path is named after him. Both are seen as memorials for the abolition of slavery.

---

[46]Retrieved from https://www.bethhaim.nl/elieser-herdenking-27-juni-2018/. Accessed on March 12, 2019.

[47]The burial register states with the name Elieser: ´moreno que foi de Paulo de Pina´, ´the brown one, which was of Paulo de Pina'. De Pina was one of the founders of the cemetery.

[48]There are different views on the meaning of the inscription and the exact status of Elieser. Was he a released slave who had converted to Judaism? Was he a dark-skinned Jew, like there were more at the time? Was he Paulo de Pina's servant? Was he a "bomb servo de deus," or a good servant of God? Retrieved from https://archief.amsterdam/stukken/dood/bom_servo_elieser/index.nl.html. Accessed on March 19, 2019.

Image 7.17. An Elaborately Decorated Seventeenth-century Grave at the Portuguese Jewish Cemetery Beth Haim in Ouderkerk aan de Amstel, Noord Holland.

Source: Photograph by Claudia Venhorst, 2018.

7.4.5. Syrian Orthodox Cemetery Glanerbrug

The Netherlands houses a Syrian Orthodox community of over 2,000 families. Most of them have settled in the region of Twente – the area around Enschede and Hengelo – in the far eastern part of the country. They came here from the 1960s as labour migrants, to work in the local textile industry. Most of them fled unstable and oppressive situations in Turkey and the Middle East. The Saint Ephrem Monastery in the tiny village of Glanerbrug is the community's spiritual and cultural centre and since 1983 has also provided a large burial facility. As Syrian Orthodox from all over Europe are buried here, and only single graves are permitted, the available burial plots filled up quickly. In 2016 a new and

Image 7.18. A Recent Grave at the Portuguese Jewish Cemetery Beth Haim in Ouderkerk aan de Amstel, Noord Holland.

Source: Photograph by Claudia Venhorst, 2018.

innovative underground burial complex, providing another 4,000 graves, was opened.[49]

7.4.6. A Variety of Muslim Burial Plots

About 25% of the municipal cemeteries in the Netherlands provide exclusive burial plots for Muslims. Although local Muslim organisations have lobbied for these dedicated plots for years, at some places the number of burials is (very) low. This has something to do with the preference of mainly first-

[49]Retrieved from https://www.ad.nl/binnenland/dorpje-bij-enschede-krijgt-groot-grafkeldercomplex-voor-syrisch-orthodoxen~a8f1ab97/. Accessed on March 19, 2019.

generation Muslims of Turkish and Moroccan descent, making up 75% of Muslims in the Netherlands, to return to their country of origin to be buried there. Those who are buried in Dutch Muslim cemeteries – generally Muslim plots on a municipal cemetery – are mainly people with strong roots in the Netherlands, like the Surinamese Javanese community and families of mixed backgrounds, and refugees who do not have the option of returning to the country of origin. Deceased children are also often buried in the Netherlands, in close proximity to their parents.

Ethnic, religious and cultural diversity among Islamic communities has inevitably led to differences in burial and burial rituals.[50] An interesting case is provided by a Muslim cemetery in the small village of Sint Michelsgestel (Brabant). In 1975, just weeks before the independence of Suriname, many Hindustani and Javanese inhabitants decided to move to the Netherlands as they foresaw a better future there. To the former contract workers that had been recruited in Java (1890–1939), it was once again a new start in a new context. In the Netherlands they were initially housed in group accommodations, and Sint Michelsgestel became their new home. After the creation of a care home for the elderly, a cemetery was established in the 1990s and accommodates demand for perpetual graves and location towards Mecca. In practice it appeared that even this specific target group of Surinamese Javanese Muslims is certainly not homogeneous as ways of thinking and personal preference vary.[51] This diversity is also expressed in a great variety of grave coverings at Muslim cemeteries across the Netherlands. Most grave coverings express the

[50]Kadrouch-Outmany, K. (2016). 'Religion at the cemetery Islamic burials in the Netherlands and Belgium'. *Contemporary Islam.* 10 (1), 87–105.
[51]Retrieved from https://www.bhic.nl/ontdekken/verhalen/javaanse-begrafenisrituelen-in-sint-michielsgestel. Accessed on March 19, 2019.

Image 7.19. Children's Grave at the Muslim Cemetery in Venlo-Blerick, Limburg.

Source: Photograph by Claudia Venhorst, 2016.

personal background of the deceased and the next of kin who maintain it: origins can be retrieved in use of certain style, language and symbols, when the deceased was in a mixed-marriage or a Dutch convert to Islam there is generally a mix of styles, when the deceased died young there are often more elaborate grave coverings and signs of extensive grave visits (Image 7.19).

CHAPTER 8

CREMATION AND CREMATORIA

8.1. HISTORIC DEVELOPMENT

By the mid-nineteenth century, preparations were made in the Netherlands to create the first national Burial Act.[1] Six drafts were written between 1855 and 1868, which evoked debate concerning the preservation (*bewaring*) and the ownership (*beschikking*) of the corpse. The fifth draft of the Act, in 1867, granted ownership to the next of kin – thereby creating a loophole for cremation – and did not explicitly exclude or prohibit cremation.[2] Moreover, the burning of corpses was mentioned as a possible form of bodily disposal in the Act's explanation:

[1]This act would also prohibit burial within churches, and within a 50-metre range of built-up areas. See Section 7.1.
[2]Franke, I. (1989). *Crematie in Nederland. 1875-1955 (pp. 12–15).* Utrecht: Matrijs.

> *The draft speaks of burial as commonly used in the country. If, however, anyone wants to order that his corpse should be burnt, then Article 1 will not stand in the way.*[3]

The possibility of modern cremation seemed at the doorstep. Yet, a convincing plea against people's ownership of the corpse by Rembertus Westerhoff, a liberal member of parliament, obstructed the road to legislation:

> *By virtue of these provisions, the persons referred to in this paragraph may, for example, desire or permit the corpse of their next of kin to be burned... to be cooked and the fleshless bones to be stored separately... According to this paragraph, one would be able to submit a seemingly dead person to the above-mentioned course of action and thus be able to kill.*[4]

The day after Westerhoff's plea, the loophole in the first article of the Burial Act was closed by Home Secretary Cornelis Fock. The new Burial Act did no longer discuss ownership, and took effect on 9 May 1869. Whereas the topic of cremation had been discussed in relation to the new Burial Act, it was yet to enter the public agenda. The Association to Introduce Cremation in the Netherlands – *De Vereeniging tot Invoering der Lijkverbranding in Nederland* – played a fundamental role in this process. Founded in 1874, and known

---

[3]Berichten en mededelingen der Vereeniging voor Facultatieve Lijkverbranding. 's-Gravenhage. 1875–1955. 1877(1), 21–22. As referred to by Franke (1989, p. 13).

[4]Gratama Hz., S. (1888). Wet tot vaststelling van bepalingen betrekkelijk het begraven van lijken, de begraafplaatsen, en de begrafenisregten van den 10-den April 1869. *Staatsblad no. 65*. 's-Gravengae. 75–76. As referred to by Franke (1989, p. 13).

as the *Koninklijke Facultatieve* today, the Association campaigned to bring this 'more advanced' form of corpse management to the attention of the Dutch. Ultimately, their goal was to make cremation a practical and legal possibility.

According to the cremationists – those in favour of cremation – cemeteries were breeding grounds for germs and epidemics to which cremation would offer a hygienic solution. Whereas the 1869 Burial Act had solved the severe threats to healthcare, some still used this argument. In addition, it was argued that cremation would result in lower cemetery maintenance and pressure on land. Such pressure has been relatively low in the Netherlands, due to the practice of clearing graves, the rapidly growing population did cause challenges, especially in urban areas. The cremationists' practical arguments were soon amplified by emotional, aesthetics and ethical concerns.[5] The best example might be the Association's propaganda posters and slogans that compared burial to cremation, in favour of the latter (Image 8.1). Burial, for example, was described as a disturbing process of bodily decay that started out with burial in the bleak Dutch weather. Cremation, by contrast, was depicted as a decent, pious and neat way of dealing with the dirty side of death.

The Association's efforts proved fruitful. In 1913 the construction of the first crematorium at the Westerveld estate in Driehuis began, and on the first of April 1914 the first cremation took place on Dutch soil – namely that of Dr C.J. Vaillant (Image 8.2). This, however, was not the first modern cremation of a Dutchman. That honour is reserved for Eduard Douwes Dekker (1820–1887), also known as

[5]Cappers, W. (1999). *Vuurproef voor een grondrecht. Koninklijke vereniging voor facultatieve crematie 1874-1999*. Zutphen: Walburg Pers, 70–81; Franke (1989, pp. 60–65); Heessels, M. (2012). *Bringing home the dead: Ritualizing cremation in the Netherlands*. Nijmegen, 18.

Image 8.1. Early Twentieth-century Cremation Propaganda of the *Vereeniging voor Facultatieve Lijkverbranding*.

Source: Archief Crematorium Westerveld, Driehuis.

Image 8.2. A Building Plan of the Westerveld Crematorium.

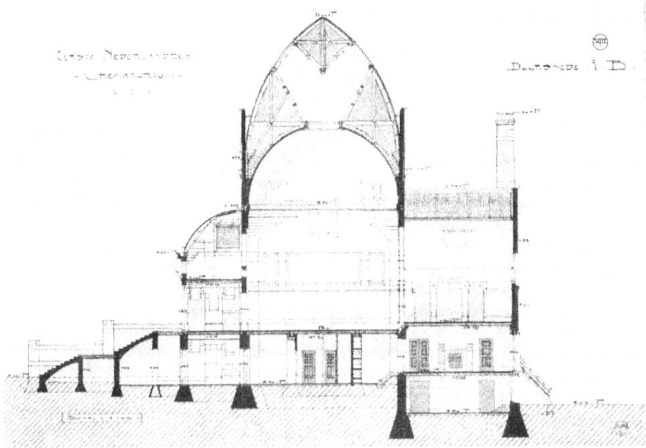

Note: Marius Poel made various designs for the first crematorium in the Netherlands.
Source: Archief Crematorium Westerveld, Driehuis.

Multatuli, the famous Dutch writer. He was cremated in Gotha, Germany. The ashes were kept by his widow until her death in 1930, and were subsequently held by the Multatuli Museum in Amsterdam. In 1948 the Koninklijke Facultatieve took the initiative to set up a monument for the first cremated Dutchman in modern history.

Now that the first crematorium had been built and the first modern cremation had taken place, the Association's campaign was no longer a matter of mere idealism. It was one of actual practice and in need of firm foothold. In addition to these early cremationists a broader societal interest in cremation emerged. In 1919, the thriving socialist agenda in the Netherlands gave rise to the Workers' Association for Cremation (AVVL) – the *Arbeiders Vereeniging Voor Lijkverbranding*. They further disseminated the cremation agenda because of its emancipatory ideals: cremation was propagated as the great equaliser. Through the Workers' Association the cremation movement now also reached the middle and working classes and membership numbers increased.[6] After the first cremation at Westerveld in 1914, the authorities prosecuted those responsible for allowing and assisting in the occurrence.[7] When the Supreme Court eventually ruled this cremation not a criminal offence, cremations were condoned but not finally legalised until 1955.

In order to achieve legislation, various forms of cremation propaganda continued throughout the 1930s. In addition to meetings and posters, writings were posted to all ministers and members of the House of Representatives.[8] Cooperation was strengthened with cremation associations elsewhere in Europe, and in 1936 both the AVVL and the Facultatieve (the Association to Introduce Cremation) joined the International Federation for Cremation. In 1940 a new proposal to change the 1869 Burial Act was discussed by the government. The Facultatieve lobbied for cremation by suggesting improvements and by protesting to the proposed changes. Also, they distributed brochures to a wide variety of national, regional and local officiants, as well as citizens.

Although discussions on legislation continued, the Second World War hindered the process. The crematorium in Velsen, for example, was temporarily closed in 1944 and plans for a second crematorium, to be built in Zwolle, were abandoned. Yet, the government had to resolve the practice of condoning cremation at some point.[9] In 1949 and 1950 the 'Kan-committee' was established to review the Burial Act, and a

[6]Franke (1989, p. 69).
[7]Cappers (1999, pp. 127–148).
[8]Franke (1989, p. 71).
[9]Franke (1989, pp. 72–75).

proposal for a new Burial Act was submitted in 1952. In the same year, plans for a new crematorium in Dieren were also approved. Subsequently a second committee led by Jan Kan (1954–1957) was set up, and cremation was legalised in the 1955 Corpse Disposal Act.[10]

In the 1960s the formal stance of the churches towards cremation changed, impacting the further rise of cremation in the Netherlands. The Roman Catholic Church had banned cremation in decrees of 1886 and 1892, reinforced in 1918 and 1925.[11] Choosing cremation had severe consequences, such as the denial of clerical services and sacraments. Both the Dutch Reformed Church and the Reformed Churches in the Netherlands had not officially embargoed the practice, but expressed a clear preference towards burial. Although this preference has continued in all churches, the General Synod of the Reformed Churches accepted cremation in 1961, and the Roman Catholic Church during the Second Vatican Council in 1963.[12] From the 1960s onwards cremation numbers grew rapidly. In 1991 burial and cremation obtained an equal legal status, and since 2003 cremation has been the dominant form of bodily disposal in the Netherlands. In 2018, 65% of the deceased were cremated (Table 8.1).

8.2. BURIAL VS CREMATION

In 2003 cremation became the most popular form of bodily disposal in the Netherlands, and research shows that ash

---

[10]Overview of administrative decisions on corpse disposal legislation since 1948. Retrieved from https://wetten.overheid.nl/BWBR0021107/2007-02-03

[11]Franke (1989, p. 43).

[12]Heessels (2012); Franke (1989, 43ff).

Table 8.1. Development of Cremation in the Netherlands.

Year	Number of Cremations	Percentage Cremated
1914	1	0
1920	177	0.2
1930	505	0.7
1940	1,061	1.2
1950	1,520	2.0
1960	3,501	4.0
1970	14,949	13.6
1980	39,947	35.0
1990	57,130	44.4
2000	68,700	48.9
2010	77,465	56.9
2018	100,089	65.3

Source: Landelijke Vereniging van Crematoria (2019). Retrieved from https://www.lvc-online.nl/aantallen

disposal is an important factor in people's choice for cremation.[13] Compared to burial, cremation offers more possibilities and flexibility as regards the post-mortem location and memorialisation of the deceased. Other reasons to choose for a cremation instead of a burial are the wishes of the deceased. Also, people indicate that the absence of grave maintenance is a significant motive. People do not want to burden their

[13]Mathijssen (2017a, p. 145).

next of kin. Interestingly, finance is seldom mentioned as a motive to opt for cremation, whereas the financial difference between burial and cremation can be quite significant. Religious motives do play a role in particular groups.

8.3. CURRENT CREMATORIUM PROVISION

The first three crematoria in the Netherlands were built in Driehuis (1913), Driebergen (1954) and Groningen (1962). After the legalisation in 1955 and corresponding with the rising cremation number in the 1970s, crematorium building increased rapidly.[14] In the last decade, the number of crematoria has again rapidly increased. Thirty-two new crematoria have been built since 2009, amounting to an increase of 36 per cent. As a result of the growing number of crematoria, the number of cremations per crematorium has begun to decrease (Table 8.2).

Both public (*gemeentelijke*) and private (*bijzondere*) crematoria exist in the Netherlands, the latter being the largest group. They are respectively run by the local authority, or by an association or a funeral insurance company. Public crematoria are open from Mondays to Saturdays, between 9 a.m. and 5 p.m. They are not obliged to offer cremation services on Sundays and public holidays, though they might decide to do so. Likewise, they might open in the evenings. Private crematoria are not legally bound by fixed opening hours.[15]

---

[14]Klaassens, M. & Groote, P. (2012). Designing a place for goodbye: The architecture of crematoria in the Netherlands. In D. Davies & C. Park (eds.). *Emotion, identity and death: Mortality across disciplines*. Farnham: Ashgate.

[15]Corpse Disposal Act, article 56.

Table 8.2. Number of Crematoria in the Netherlands.

Year	Number of Crematoria	Number of Cremations per Crematorium
1913 (Velsen)	1	1
1954 (Driebergen)	2	–
1962 (Groningen)	3	–
1988	32	–
2009	68	1,120
2014	80	1,068
2015	85	1,096
2016	93	1,010
2017	100	967

Source: UitvaartBranchemonitor (2018). *Stand van de uitvaartbranche 2017*. Den Haag: Uitvaartmedia; Landelijke Vereniging van Crematoria (2019). Retrieved from https://www.lvc-online.nl/leden

8.4. CREMATORIUM ARCHITECTURE

Four phases of crematorium design have been identified in the Netherlands.[16] The first crematorium in Driehuis (1913) was designed by Marius Poel and was built in a *pre-modern* style with a dome as its central feature (Images 2.2 and 8.2). It was commissioned by the Facultatieve, who wanted a building without neo-gothic and traditional religious elements to reflect their progressive ideology. During the second phase, between

[16]Klaassens and Groote (2012).

1930 and 1970, *shake-hands modernism* – a soft version of modernism – entered crematorium architecture.[17] Buildings were functional but left room for aesthetics, without the brutality of post-war modernist architecture. Also nature began to play an increasingly important role in crematorium design. Examples are the crematorium in Driebergen (1954) designed by H. C. P. Nuyten, the crematorium in Groningen (1962) designed by A. H. Wegerif and the Ockenburg crematorium in The Hague (1968) designed by Jan Wils. From the 1970s onwards, large-scale technological designs with production-oriented goals were increasingly criticised. Crematoria became smaller. Yet, the renewed attention for social and human goals did not always turn out as planned. The *sub-modern* architecture of crematoria was often so downgraded that places emerged without any symbolic value or meaning. Some crematoria in this era have been described as low quality, indistinctive and unemotional places.[18] From the 1990s onwards, and especially in the twenty-first century, the outlook of crematorium buildings became *post-modern.* From being non-places, crematoria were transformed into unique buildings with a renewed attention to place.[19] Designs became more outspoken and focused on new materials, experimental routings, cultural diversity and environmental concerns. Many crematoria were also refurbished in view of this. Examples are De Nieuwe Ooster in Amsterdam (refurbished in 2007),

---

[17]Klaassens and Groote (2012, p. 124); Colenbrander, B. W. (1993). *Style: Standard and signature in Dutch architecture of the nineteenth and twentieth centuries.* Rotterdam: Nai Publishers.

[18]Hekkema, H. (2002). Uitvaartcultuur als ontwerpopgave; De oesters zijn gegeten, de witte wijn is gedronken. In H. Hekkema (ed.). *Uitvaartcultuur als ontwerpopgave: Situering en architectuur van funeraire functies in een veranderende samenleving; een ideeeënprijsvraag voor studenten* (pp. 59–76). Zwolle: Esselink Stichting.

[19]Klaassens and Groote (2012).

the Yardenhuis in Amsterdam (under construction) and Crematorium Ommeland en Stad in Groningen (2018) which follows BREEAM sustainability guidelines.[20]

8.5. CREMATION LAW AND CERTIFICATION

Cremation practice is defined by the Corpse Disposal Act – *de Wet op de Lijkbezorging*. This Act originates in the 1869 Burial Act. When cremation became a legal practice in 1955 the name of the Act changed and a chapter on cremation was added. The Act was again significantly amended and modernised in 1991 when cremation acquired the same legal status as burial.[21] It then became possible for the bereaved to take the ashes of their deceased home. In 1998, an adjustment followed that officially allowed people to divide the ashes into parts, and thus to scatter them or divide them over different urns. The fourth chapter of the Corpse Disposal Act describes the procedures that must be followed to ensure that the cremation is practically safe and ethically informed. The chapter lays down six requirements:

> First, the law prescribes that the cremation must take place in the crematorium, and cannot take place in the open air. The crematorium owner must register all cremations.
>
> Second, the cremation cannot take place before 36 hours after death, nor can it take place later than six working days after death. Under special circumstances, this period can be shortened or extended. To shorten the period, the public

[20]Retrieved from https://www.breeam.com/. Accessed on April 15, 2019.

[21]Additional practices that were required in the case of cremation, but that were deemed non-functional, such as the involvement of a second medical doctor, were then removed from the Act.

persecutor must be asked for an exemption. To extend the period, a request must be made at the local authority.

Third, the cremation can only take place after two forms have been signed by a medical doctor: The *A-statement* and the *B-statement*. The A-statement gives an overview of the personal information of the deceased and the date of death. When doubts exist regarding the cause of death or when a minor has died, this must be indicated on the form and a second municipal independent physician must be consulted. Also a stillbirth must be indicated separately on the form. The A-statement is usually issued by the funeral director (through the next of kin might do this as well) who takes it to the local authority to register the death, after which the leave to cremate (or bury) the deceased is issued. The leave of the local authority is needed to conduct the cremation. The B-statement describes the specific cause of death. It can be an extensive document that indicates the illness or injury that led to death and the circumstances that led to death. A distinction is made between natural death, non-natural death and stillbirth. The B-statement is sent to the Central Bureau for Statistics (CBS) after completion, and is used to compile national mortality statistics.

Fourth, the cremation can only take place when the registration number attached to the coffin matches the number on the paperwork. Subsequently, these two numbers must match the number attached to the ash box. To make this identification process easy, refractory identification stones are used in crematoria. The registration number is engraved in the stone and checked with the paperwork of the deceased before cremation. The stone is cremated together with the deceased, but survives the cremation. It thus identifies the cremated remains.

After the cremulation process, the identification stone is placed in the ash box together with the deceased's ashes.

Fifth, the crematorium owner is obliged by law to safeguard the ashes (held in a box) on the crematorium premises for at least one month. This one-month waiting period is unique in Europe. It finds it origins in late nineteenth century Leiden where Maria Catharina Swanenburg – nicknamed Goeie Mie – poisoned her own family (Image 8.3). It was feared that criminal cases like Maria's would remain unresolved or worse, that they could be covered up by cremating the victims. Therefore, a one-month waiting period was proposed and installed. This period was thought to allow forensic investigation in case of suspicious circumstances. Although the ashes are not a fruitful source for forensics, the waiting period has become part of formal legislation. Today it is interpreted by funeral professionals as a waiting period for the bereaved, granting them time to reflect upon the ash disposal.

Sixth, at least one month after the cremation, the crematorium owner releases the ashes (*asuitgifte*). S/he must facilitate the final placement of the ash container (*asbus*), or the scattering of the ashes at the crematorium grounds or another assigned place. The ash container can also be handed over to the next of kin. Alternatively, the ash container can be repatriated or send abroad (see Section 3.2.2).

8.5.1. Current Legal Debates

The Corpse Disposal Act develops over time in view of changing needs and wishes. Changes to the Act have been proposed in 2018, based on survey research and expert consultation with funeral professionals and researchers.

Image 8.3. The Leiden Murderess Maria Catharina Swanenburg

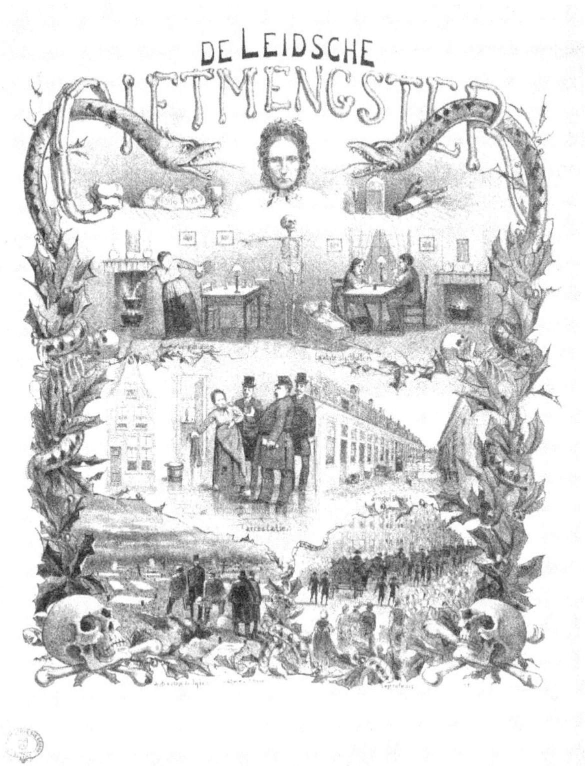

Note: Maria Swanenburg's case influenced cremation discussions in the Netherlands, resulting in the instalment of a one-month waiting period to retrieve the ashes of the deceased from the crematorium.
Source: Image by Roelof Raar, 1883.

These are currently part of parliamentary discussions (see Sections 3.3. and 3.3.1).[22] The most important changes that are subject to debate in view of cremation are the following:

- allow the ashes – for instance of partners – to be mixed, to make it possible to scatter or keep the ashes together;
- remove the one-month waiting period to retrieve the ashes from the crematorium;
- allow stillborn twins, as well as a mother and baby who have died in labour, to be buried or cremated together (in the same coffin);
- extend the period within which the funeral must take place from six to eight working days;
- allow burial or cremation to take place 20 hours after death, instead of 36 hours;
- create new possibilities for bodily disposal (cryomation, resomation and compostation);
- make arrangements for ashes that are left at the crematorium; and
- create one set of forms for cremation and burial, instead of two.

8.6. CREMATORIUM LOGISTICS

Typically, crematoria can be found at the outskirts of cities and towns, as is defined in the municipal development plan.

---

[22]D66 (2018). Initiatiefnota Moderne Uitvaartwet. Retrieved from https://d66.nl/content/uploads/sites/2/2018/11/Initiatiefnota-Moderne-Uitvaartwet.pdf

About one-third of the Dutch crematories is situated on or near cemetery grounds.[23] Often there are possibilities for ash disposal on site, or on the neighbouring cemetery ground. At the crematorium grounds, there are parking facilities for both bicycles and cars, and there is a separate parking area for employees. The crematorium building typically consists of a main entrance, an employee entrance and a welcoming hall. Usually a separate entrance is located at the back or to the side of the building for the hearse, through which the deceased can be brought to the auditorium. The building usually has two auditoria in which cremation services can be held, a family waiting room, a cremator room, a cremulator or technical room, a storage room for the cremated remains, a storage room for funeral props and tools, a technical music room, offices kitchen facilities for employees, tea and coffee making facilities for mourners, restrooms, and a bar or restaurant.

8.6.1. Welcoming Facilities at the Crematorium

At the day of the cremation, mourners enter the crematorium through the *main entrance*, which leads to a welcoming hall or restaurant. The *welcoming hall* is typically designed as a large empty space, decorated only by a few couches or chairs, carpets, some plants and a coffee machine. Here, people await the start of the funeral service. Sometimes, the welcoming hall also functions as a restaurant or bar where the mourners may gather for a traditional *koffietafel* (coffee and cake), drinks, snacks or food after the funeral services. The space is then decorated with tables, chairs and a bar. When used as a

---

[23]Retrieved from https://www.begraafplaats.nl/de-begraafplaats/artikel/ook-een-crematorium/. Accessed on April 11, 2019.

waiting room, the bars are usually closed. Yet, there will be staff nearby and mourners will be able to get a glass of water or coffee. In the welcoming area, there are also restrooms available and (moveable) coat racks.

It is common for the crematorium to have a separate *family waiting room*. Here the closest family can await the start of the funeral service. This room also contains couches, chairs, carpets, tables, coffee facilities and usually a kitchen, plants, paintings and private restrooms. This room often has a separate entrance from the outside of the crematorium building, and thus can be privately accessed. Of course it can also be accessed from within. In some crematoria it is possible for the deceased to stay with the next of kin in the family room.

In the period before the funeral, the deceased usually remains at the funeral home or is laid out at home. Yet, some crematoria provide cooled *mourning rooms* on site. These rooms are not simply functional: they are decorated, for instance with paintings and warm light, and – very significantly – can be further adorned by the next of kin with flowers, candles, or personal objects. Attached to the cooled room usually is a *visiting room*. This room is at a regular temperature and can be used by the mourners who want to leave the cooled room or do not want to enter it. The visiting room is also decorated with furniture, and often supplied with a kitchenette and restrooms. In many cases this area can be accessed 24/7 by the immediate mourners in the period before the funeral. Mourning room facilities can also be found in funeral homes.

8.6.2. Cremation Services in the Auditorium

The cremation service takes place in the auditorium (*aula*). Services usually last for 45 minutes, and it is possible to book a double slot in the auditorium for an extra fee. An extra fee may also be charged when one runs over time. Furthermore, there is a 15-minute break between services to clear and clean the auditorium for the next funeral.

Crematoria usually have two auditoriums, a larger and smaller one, which accommodate different sizes of funerals. The buildings are often designed to accommodate overspill as well as small groups of mourners. The welcoming area can normally become part of the auditorium space, and has audio and video facilities. Spaces can also be made smaller, and in recent years, special rooms have been created for small scale funerals. These rooms are decorated like a large living room with an open kitchen and a seating area around the deceased where the ceremony can take place. The space aims to facilitate a personal, informal and intimate farewell (Image 8.4).

When a crematorium has multiple auditoria, this impacts on the routing of mourners through the building. When the mourners enter the crematorium through one main entrance, the timing and routing of services becomes very important and the different auditoria usually have their own waiting area to avoid a mingling of mourners. It is also common that the different auditoria each have their own parking area and entrance.

The auditorium is typically decorated with comfortable couches or chairs for the mourners, a catafalque in front, candles next to or embedded in the catafalque, and a music installation. The crematorium space does not resemble a church building. There usually is some art and there might be plants too. It is common to have video or wide screen facilities. In addition, the auditorium might have extra facilities such as an organ or a piano.

The auditorium space is – to a larger or lesser extent – decorated by the next of kin or the funeral director before the start of the funeral. People can adorn the coffin and the

Image 8.4. Small Auditorium at a Crematorium in Gelderland.

Note: This room also accommodates more informal funeral gatherings.
Source: Photograph by Brenda Mathijssen, 2017.

catafalque, place pictures and bring additional attributes such as plants, candles and artworks.

Auditoria do not tend to have fixed religious iconography. Instead, portable religious icons are used, depending on the particular funeral wishes (Image 6.4). In some cases, natural or regional symbols have gained a fixed place in the crematorium design, often swapping places with former religious ones. This could be a sun on a wall instead of a cross, or a wall-size cityscape picture. Whereas not religious, these decorations are not neutral and they are not appreciated by all mourners. They reflect an increasingly diverse society in which symbols must be reinvented and adjusted to be meaningful to diverse groups of mourners. This continues to be a challenge for contemporary crematoria.

8.6.3. Crematoria and Funeral Music

Crematoria have provided space for new funeral music repertoires in the Netherlands. Where funeral music long consisted of traditional religious songs, such as hymns performed by a choir, contemporary funerals are characterised by an eclectic mixture of musical genres, from pop to rock to classical, from the Netherlands and abroad (see Section 6.4.6). Whereas popular music is not accepted in all religious buildings, crematoria have long provided professional facilities.

8.6.4. Incineration and the Witnessing of the Charge

Broadly speaking, the funeral service at a crematorium can end in two different ways. First, it is common for the mourners to say *farewell to the deceased in the auditorium*. The more distant relatives and friends are typically the first to rise from their seats to walk passed the coffin. They pay their last respects to the deceased by touching the coffin or nodding towards it, and then walk to the exit of the auditorium. The exit usually leads to the restaurant area. It is common for the closest next of kin to stay behind in the auditorium to pay their last respects privately. They may gather around the deceased to say farewell or there might be a final tribute before they walk away from the deceased and leave the auditorium. After the service, when the mourners have left the auditorium, the crematorium employees remove the deceased from the auditorium on a wheeled bier to the cremator room. The mourners typically gather for a (type of) coffee-table in the crematorium restaurant or elsewhere.

Second, the closest mourners may say *farewell to the deceased in the cremator room* and *witness and/or initiate the charge*.[24] In the last two decades, this has become common practice in the Dutch context. If capacity allows, the next of kin might remove the deceased from the auditorium on a wheeled bier to the cremator room at the end of the service. This can be done with all mourners present or in small company, and crematorium employees or the funeral director may assist the next of kin. If capacity does not allow, there might be a time gap between the service and the actual cremation. The service in the auditorium then ends as described above, and the next of kin return to the cremator room to witness the charge at a later moment that day. The cremator rooms have undergone drastic refurbishments in the last two decades to make them more accessible to the bereaved. Often the walls have been painted in warm colours or have been decorated with poetry, and plants paintings and furniture (Image 8.5).

The design of the crematorium building impacts the deceased's journey to the cremator, and thereby may impact the funeral ritual. When the cremator room is located next to the auditorium, which is often the case, the journey is straightforward. In some cases, it is possible for the coffin to descend into the floor at the end of the service, resembling the process of burial. This is often merely symbolic, which means that the deceased still has to come back up to be removed to the cremator room by professionals. Yet, sometimes the journey to the cremator is more exceptional. At De Nieuwe Ooster in Amsterdam the cremator is situated on the first floor, whereas the auditorium is based at the ground level. Because of the monumental status of the building and the wall paintings

---

[24]It has been argued that the discomfort of walking away from the deceased – and leave him or her to be guided to the cremator by the professionals – has sparked the trend to witness the charge, see Mathijssen (2017a).

Image 8.5. Witnessing the Charge of the Deceased at a Crematorium in Gelderland.

Source: Photograph by Claudia Venhorst, 2016.

within the building, this was the only suitable layout for the refurbishment process that took place in 2007. As a result, the coffin now must go up at the end of the service. Mourners can choose to witness this process, which has created (unexpected) opportunities for symbolism. 'Stairway to Heaven' has become a popular song to play when the deceased ascends, and interestingly, the number of people who want to witness the charge after the service has decreased. This suggests that the symbolism of the ascending coffin provides a fitting closure to the next of kin.

8.6.5. The Crematorium Bar and Restaurant

People typically gather for a coffee-table, traditionally consisting of coffee and cake, or for food and drinks after the funeral service. This can be organised in the crematorium restaurant. Crematoria usually provide elaborate catering, resembling the quality of any other decent restaurant or pub. Alternatively, people may prefer to go home instead, or may visit another restaurant or pub.

8.6.6. The Technical Cremation Process

The actual cremation process is fully automated by a computer system, regulating time and heat, and lasts for 70–90 minutes, depending on the coffin and the weight of deceased. The environmental chamber of the cremator is preheated to 820 degrees Celsius in the morning, before the first cremation takes places. When the coffin enters the cremator, the heat will rise to a set temperature of approximately 1,100 degrees Celsius. A computer keeps track of what is happening and ensures that the correct temperatures are achieved to create an optimal cremation process.

Each crematorium has at least one employee who can operate the cremator, called the cremator operator (*ovenist*). S/he ensures that the coffin enters the cremator correctly, checks the registration number and the identification stone, and monitors the process. When the next of kin are present at the beginning of the cremation, the *ovenist* explains the cremation procedures to them, and may help them to initiate the charge if they wish to do so.

After the cremation, the operator removes the cremated remains. A shaft in the oven is opened and the cremated remains are swept to the front of the oven. Via the shaft the cremated remains land in an ash pan (*aspan*) in the bottom of the cremator. The shaft is then closed and the cremator space is clean to be used for the next cremation (Images 8.6 and 8.7).

In some crematoria, the last deceased of the day stays overnight in the ash pan of the cremator. S/he is called 'the sleeper'. The cremated remains cool down in the evening and are removed the next morning.

8.6.7. Environmental Regulations

The environmental requirements of crematoria are described in the Decree on environmental management – *het Activiteitenbesluit milieubeheer*.[25] This decree concerns crematoria for humans as well as animals, and scatter sites for ashes. It discusses both soil and air regulations. The soil regulations prescribe that the soil quality of scatter fields must be tested periodically. If alternating scatter fields are used – which means that one field is in use, whereas the other observes a 10-year rest period – the frequency of tests depends on actual use. When over 370 scatterings take place per hectare per year, the first soil test takes place within three months and then every five years. When there are between 90 and 370 scatterings, the test is repeated every 25 years. If fewer than 90 scatterings take place, no soil tests are required. The crematorium must meet the omission standard of 1,000 mg of phosphate per m^2 per year, and may not exceed this amount. Only a person or an institution that is recognised by the Soil Quality Decree may conduct soil investigations and leaching tests. The design of the soil investigation must comply with NEN 5740. If it appears

[25]The regulations that are summarised in this section can be accessed via https://www.infomil.nl/onderwerpen/integrale-regels/activiteitenbesluit/activiteiten/crematorium/

Image 8.6. The Technical Cremation Process: The Operator Removes the Cremated Remains.

Source: Photograph taken by Claudia Venhorst, 2015.

Image 8.7. The Technical Cremation Process: After Cremulation the Ashes Are Placed in Ash Containers for Storage.

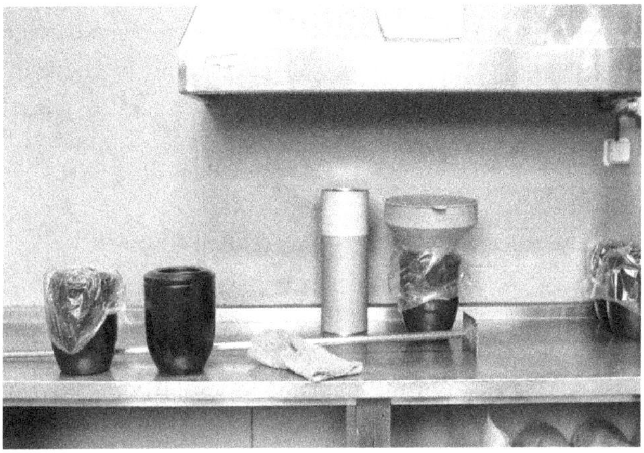

Source: Photograph taken by Claudia Venhorst, 2015.

that the soil quality has deteriorated, the installation owner must restore the quality. The Decree on environmental management also regulates the number of scatterings, and prescribes that the ashes must be evenly distributed when scattered and cannot drift outside of the scatterfield.

Crematoria also are subject to air regulations. Metal and plastic items must be removed before cremation and the coffin or covering may not be of lead or zinc. The cremation oven must meet the requirements for inspection and maintenance: proper combustion, NOx, mercury (not for animal crematoria), dioxins and furans, and dust (only for animal crematoria). The temperature must always be higher than 800°C, and therefore the cremator must be equipped with an automatic control. The crematorium must also continuously monitor the oxygen levels, to indicate whether the cremation oven is functioning properly. The oxygen level in the after-burning room must be at least 6 per cent. A short-term exceedance is permitted, but may not be lower than 3 per cent and not longer than one minute. Six months after commissioning, the proper functioning of the installation must be checked by an expert for example an installer. This check is repeated annually, and recorded in a logbook.

8.6.8. Cremulation and Ash Storage

After being removed from the cremator, the cremated remains are treated in the ash processing room. This room is often separated from the cremator room. Here the cremated remains cool down further, and the remaining orthopaedic implants and metals are removed using a strong magnet. Subsequently, the cremated remains are cremulated. The ashes and bones are being placed in a drum to be granulated by metal balls. The residue are the 'ashes' and these are boxed and placed in a storage room (Image 8.8). The ashes will stay there for at least one month, as prescribed by the Dutch Corpse Disposal Act.

8.7. THE ASHES

8.7.1. Retrieving the Ashes

From one month after the cremation onwards, the next of kin can retrieve the ashes of their deceased from the crematorium. They are informed about this during the funeral preparations, and receive a letter from the crematorium a few weeks after the cremation. People may wait to retrieve the ashes, for instance

Image 8.8. The Ash Storage Room.

Source: Photograph by Claudia Venhorst, 2015.

because they have not yet chosen a form of ash disposal, or because they feel uncomfortable to bring the ashes home.

In legal terms only one family member has the responsibility over the retrieval and the subsequent disposal of the ashes: the client who has ordered the cremation. This is the person who has signed the paperwork during the funeral preparations. Whereas people tend to decide upon the ash retrieval and disposal together with their relatives, this can be a potential source for conflict and family disputes.

The ash retrieval itself is usually handled by the office employees at the crematorium, and takes place in a separate room – the client office – or in a separate office building on the crematorium premises. It can be a challenging process for the next of kin, who often have not visited the crematorium since the funeral and who do not know what to expect. Upon arrival, the funeral professionals offer coffee and tea to the next of kin. Then the practical details are discussed and the legal forms are signed. Because it is impossible to predict the reaction of the next of kin, the ashes are only brought in when the paperwork has been completed.[26]

The ashes are placed in a standard box, and usually weigh between 2 and 3 kg. They can also be transferred to an urn: the room were the ash retrieval takes place is sometimes filled with examples of urns and ash objects that can be purchased by the next of kin.

8.7.2. Types of Ash Disposal

The amendments of the Corpse Disposal Act in the 1990s, which granted permission to take the cremated remains home

[26]Venhorst and Mathijssen (2017).

and to divide them into parts, impacted the creation of urns, scatter tubes, ash objects, ash jewellery, ash paintings and ash tattoos. Today, the majority of people in the Netherlands scatter the ashes of their deceased. Officially, one must obtain permission of the land owner to scatter ashes at a particular location. In practice, however, people tend to scatter the ashes at any location that is deemed socially appropriate. In some cases, this might result in problems or complaints at the local crematorium or police. Crematorium owners, for example, are occasionally asked to remove the wrongfully scattered cremated remains or to contact the next of kin to do so.

In addition to scattering, it is common in the Netherlands to lease an urn grave at the cemetery or to keep an urn at home. Sometimes people have small urns that can be divided among the next of kin. Also, it is common to create an ash object or to incorporate ashes in jewellery. Moreover, many people ask the crematorium professionals to dispose of the ashes at the crematorium grounds or at sea (Image 8.9). Crematoria may also dispose ashes when the next of kin have not retrieved them after several years. They maintain a record of the disposals, in case next of kin enquire at a later stage.

8.7.3. Ash Artists and Entrepreneurs

Although scattering and urn graves are much valued and common in the Netherlands, creative entrepreneurs and artists continue to develop new products and procedures for ash disposal. To give an impression of this flourishing market, we have selected a few products that have been designed in the Netherlands or have entered the market in recent years.

Image 8.9. Ash Scattering Garden at Crematorium Blerick, Limburg.

Source: Photograph by Claudia Venhorst, 2016.

Commonplace in the Netherlands and abroad are the 'Bios Urns' or 'Bios Incubes', a green form of ash disposal that has been developed by a start-up company in Barcelona, Spain.[27] The urn and incube are made of biodegradable materials and allow the planting of a tree or plant with the ashes of the deceased. Two Dutch initiatives that resemble the Bios Urn are 'Remember in Green' and 'My Tree' (*Mijn boom*).[28] These companies assist the next of kin in choosing a typical tree, and in planting it together with ashes of the deceased to create a living monument.

[27]Retrieved from https://www.biologische-urn.nl. Accessed on March 5, 2019.

[28]Retrieved from https://rememberingreen.nland http://www.mijn-boom.nl. Accessed on March 5, 2019.

In a country that is dominated and shaped by water, a water urn of course has entered the market. Having enough space to incorporate the ashes of two people, the 'Water Urn' brings the ashes into contact with rainwater.[29] Over a period of circa 10 years, the ashes are gradually removed together with the rainwater and absorbed by the groundwater. Also, floating urns exist that can be placed on lakes or ponds.

Another green ash disposal innovation is the so-called TOLAD (Totem of Life and Death).[30] Designed by a Dutch company from Nijmegen, the TOLAD is a walking stick that drops a little bit of ashes, ca. 10 g, as you walk with it. Step by step, it facilitates the scattering of the ashes of the deceased. Because of its shape and function, the TOLAD can be handed over to be shared with multiple friends and family members.

Today, ashes can be incorporated in an infinite number of objects which continue to be designed and developed by artists and entrepreneurs. Ceramics, glass, metal and wood are all used to create memorial objects which can be placed in people's homes or gardens. Several artists in the Netherlands also use the ashes in their abstract or portrait paintings, or in their tattoos.

8.7.4. Accommodating Hindu Ash Disposal

In 2006 the intercultural ash scattering field 'Nirvana' opened in Usselo, Overijssel. The area has been developed in collaboration with the regional Hindu community, and is designed to accommodate ash scatterings following Hindu ritual

[29]Retrieved from https://waterurn.nl. Accessed on March 5, 2019.
[30]Retrieved from https://www.tolad-one.com. Accessed on March 5, 2019.

practices.[31] Within Hinduism, it is believed that the body consists of five main elements: water, air, ether, fire and earth. After death, these elements must return to their original source as soon as possible. Therefore, the body is cremated and immediately scattered above floating water.[32] At the Usselo cemetery, a water stream has been created in view of these needs, and during the opening of the scatterfield, water from the Ganges was poured into the local stream to symbolically and literally connect the two. In this way, a 'local Ganges' emerged.

8.8. CREMATION EQUIPMENT AND ORTHOMETALS

Dutch companies play a role in the international market of cremation technology and equipment. The Facultatieve Group, for instance, is the world market leader in the field of cremation incinerators, filters, cremators and installations.[33] Another important company that is leaving a footprint – or rather tries to reduce it – is OrthoMetals, founded in 1997 in the town of Meppel.[34] OrthoMetals recycles orthopaedic implants and other metals – such as hip implants and fillings – that remain after cremation (Image 8.10). Rather than being seen as waste, they are picked up and recycled by OrthoMetals free of charge. The company works together with 700 crematoria in 20 countries. After deducting their

[31]Swhajor, A., Heessels, M., Van der Velde, P. & Venbrux, E. (2010). Aan de Ganges in Twente. Onderhandelen over vormgeven van hindoedodenrituelen in Nederland. *Quotidian. Dutch Journal for the Study of Everyday Life*. 2, 83–102.

[32]Parry, J. P. (1994). *Death in Banaras*. Cambridge: Cambridge University Press.

[33]Retrieved from https://facultatieve.com. Accessed on March 5, 2019.

[34]Retrieved from https://orthometals.com. Accessed on March 5, 2019.

Image 8.10. Buckets Collecting Ortho Materials for Recycling.

Source: Photograph taken at a Crematorium in Gelderland by Claudia Venhorst, 2017.

operating expenses, the majority of the profit goes back to the crematoria and is used for national trusts. In the Netherlands, this money benefits the Dr C. J. Vaillant Fund, the charity fund of the National Association of Crematoria (LVC), which supports a large number of national and regional initiatives.

CHAPTER 9

DEATH AND REMEMBRANCE IN THE PUBLIC SPHERE

9.1. PERSONAL COMMEMORATION: BETWEEN PRIVATE AND PUBLIC

How people are commemorated and by whom depends on who died, the circumstances of death and the relationship between the deceased and those left behind. Deceased relatives and friends are remembered at private memorials at home, at cemeteries and at other memorial sites. Such sites are often situated between the private and the public, where both the immediate relatives and bystanders engage. The importance of memorialisation and the value of memorial sites is reflected in a wide variety of commemorative practices.

Having a memorial to visit is often mentioned as one of the advantages of burial. The cemetery is a place for the dead as well as for the living. It is a place where the bereaved can maintain, reconfigure and materialise their relationship with the deceased. People spend a lot of care, attention, effort and money on decorating the grave. Although grave visits are private and personal to a certain extent, they are also public. They occur in the public setting of a cemetery, a different setting than private memorials that are set up at home.

Cemeteries also continue to be commemorative sites for those without a grave. Memorial gardens have been installed, and in the past decades over 160 monuments for stillborn children have been erected, mainly on cemetery grounds and crematorium premises across the country.[1] Also in public spaces, commemorative practices and memorials can be observed. Ash dispersals are performed in gardens, parks, beaches and city and town centres. Shrines or road side memorials are common in both urban and rural landscapes. In the absence of an actual grave or in the case of a tragic death, these monuments are a place for personal commemoration.

9.1.1. All Souls' Day

All Souls' Day, the original Catholic tradition of collectively commemorating the deceased on 2 November, is usually celebrated with a requiem mass. The graves are cleaned and then decorated with flowers and candles. In the Netherlands this type of tradition has only been practised in the margins. However, at the beginning of the twenty-first century, there has been a rediscovery of All Souls'. New collective forms of remembrance have been developed and are performed outside of church institutions, often at cemeteries. Here, the deceased are remembered through a variety of reinvented practices. In 2005 artist Ida van der Lee started 'Allerzielen Alom', an initiative that 'hospitably decorated cemeteries with light, sound

[1]Faro, L. M. C. (2015). Postponed, monuments in the Netherlands: Manifestation, context, and meaning. S.l.: [s.n.].M173.

and art'.[2] In subsequent years more cemeteries joined her initiative, or started their own commemorative event.[3] In November, local cemeteries typically organise events such as small concerts, remembrance services or guided tours. In 2008 the public broadcasting company KRO – Katholieke Radio Omroep – initiated a theme week on remembrance with both on- and off-screen programming. The week was called 'Ode to the Dead' (*Ode aan de doden*), and the different events and activities focused on public figures and ordinary people who had passed away during the year. The media campaign 'Who do you light a candle for?' provided a popular platform for people to share their personal story of loss. Since 2008, the week has been repeated yearly. It usually concludes with a live broadcast from a cemetery or church where a contemporary All Souls' celebration is taking place.

A similar project that has gained popularity in the Netherlands is Worldwide Candle Lighting Day (*Wereldlichtjesdag*). This day started as an online initiative in 1997 in the USA to honour children who lived tragically short lives for a number of reasons.[4] The original call was to light a candle at home on the second Sunday in December at 7 p.m. Doing so in different time zones would allow a 24-hour wave of light to spread across the globe, offering consolation and solidarity to the bereaved. Today, hundreds of formal and informal lighting ceremonies are held, also in the Netherlands.

---

[2]Maaker E. de, Venbrux E. & Quartier T. (2011). Reinventing "All Souls' Day": Spirituality, contemporary art, and the remembrance of the dead. In A. Gregor (Ed.). *Ritual dynamics and the science of ritual. Reflexivity, media and visuality* (pp. 617–634). Wiesbaden: Harrassowitz Verlag.

[3]Hoondert, M. & Arfman, W. (2013). Musicalising All Souls' Day rituals. *Yearbook for Ritual and Liturgical Studies*. 29, 113–131.

[4]Retrieved from https://www.compassionatefriends.org/event/22nd-annual-worldwide-candle-lighting/. Accessed on March 16, 2019.

What once was a private commemoration is now picked up by local bereavement groups, churches, funeral homes, hospitals, hospices, schools, cemeteries and community centres. During local ceremonies the lighting of candles is often accompanied by reading the children's names (Image 9.1).

9.1.2. Virtual Commemoration

Internet and social media have impacted on funerary announcements and the ways in which people remember the dead. Obituaries and death announcements used to be sent by mail, or were printed in a (local) newspaper. Today they are increasingly published online with a much wider and public outreach. The internet also offers a variety of remembrance websites and platforms. Many emerge directly as a result of a death, and become non-active or disappear within a relatively

Image 9.1. A Commemoration Tree at an All Souls' Event.

Note: Message reads: 'Do you also think of us? We still think of you a lot. Love'.
Source: Photograph by Claudia Venhorst at the Moscowa Cemetery Arnhem, 2015.

short timeframe. Virtual cemeteries have emerged, dedicated condolence websites have been built and 'dead' profiles exist on Facebook. On the website Condoleance.nl people can set up an online condolence registers to which others can easily respond. The site was initiated after the tragic Volendam New Year's Fire in 2001 and was a way for a broad public to express condolences for the victims. The site has since then been used for private as well as national registers. Another website is Mensenlinq.nl, where death announcements published in printed newspapers become available online. The website offers people the opportunity to respond, add an in memoriam and post personal videos.

In addition, a wide range of blogs and digital communities has emerged enabling people to share stories of loss and mourning. They cover experiences of loss in general or include specific groups, for instance for stillbirths, pet deaths or bereft (grand)parents. Moreover, a large number of memorial clips is uploaded to YouTube, and the comments section is widely used to commemorate lost loved ones as well as the famous deceased.

9.2. WAR AND HOLOCAUST COMMEMORATION

9.2.1. National Remembrance of the Dead: May 4

Since 1947, the Netherlands commemorates its war victims on the 4th of May during the National Remembrance of the Dead (*Dodenherdenking*). It is the most public and the only official commemoration ceremony in the country.[5] Despite

[5]Retrieved from https://www.4en5mei.nl/herdenken-en-vieren/veelgestelde-vragen/achtergrondinformatie-herdenken/geschiedenis. Accessed on March 16, 2019.

the varied experiences of people during the war, all victims are jointly commemorated. As a country we reflect upon the horrors of war, such as violence, the Holocaust, the genocide on Roma and Sinti, internment, lack of freedom, terror, arbitrariness and resistance. Since 1961, we commemorate:

> *all Dutch war victims – civilians and soldiers – who died or were killed in the Kingdom of the Netherlands or anywhere in the world since the outbreak of the Second World War, as well as in later war situations and during peace operations.*[6]

Traditionally the main ceremony takes place at the National Monument on Dam Square in Amsterdam, and it is broadcasted on television and radio. The ceremony is attended by members of Parliament and the Royal family, military leaders, representatives of the resistance movement and other social groups. At 20:00 hours, two minutes of silence are observed throughout the country. Public transport and other traffic is stopped. In many towns throughout the country people are invited to observe the two minutes of silence together at a local monument. They listen to speeches, and lay down flowers to remember the dead. Remembrance Day is followed by an abundant celebration of Liberation Day on the 5th of May.

9.2.2. Holocaust Names Memorial

In 2015 the Auschwitz Committee Netherlands announced that a Holocaust Name Memorial would be erected in Amsterdam. The monument would hold the first and last

[6]Retrieved from https://www.4en5mei.nl/herdenken-en-vieren/veelgestelde-vragen/achtergrondinformatie-herdenken/wie-herdenken-we/wat-is-het-memorandum. Accessed on March 16, 2019.

name of 102.000 Dutch Holocaust victims, as well as their date of birth, and their age at the time of death. Although the victims of the Holocaust are commemorated at a number of places, the Committee argued that a central monument with the names of all Dutch victims is needed.

After they announced their plans, intense and widely mediatised discussions arose that questioned the need for such a monument. The initiators stressed the importance of a monument that would commemorate all victims together and each victim individually, particularly because most victims never had a personal gravesite that the surviving relatives could visit. Furthermore, the Committee emphasised the educational and symbolic function of the memorial. The large number of names would function as a lasting reminder of the horrors that people had to endure, and the monument would be a warning for the possible consequences of racial hatred, discrimination and war violence.[7]

So far, however, the initiators have been unsuccessful. The biggest point of contestation is the precise location of the monument. Local residents have spoken out against 'the wall with names' because it would be too colossal for the small park for which it was initially planned. The municipality of Amsterdam did find a more suitable location, but again the local residents protested as 24 trees had to be removed. At the moment the building of the memorial has been delayed.

9.2.3. Honour Fields and War Cemeteries

Throughout the Netherlands, military fields of honour have been established for soldiers of the allied forces who died in

[7]Retrieved from https://www.holocaustnamenmonument.nl/nl/home/. Accessed on March 16, 2019.

the liberation of the Netherlands have been buried here. The largest military cemeteries are found in Oosterbeek (1,754 graves), Nijmegen (1,543), Groesbeek (2,617) and Margraten (8,302). The fields of honour of the allied forces are recognisable by the typical design of the numerous, identical gravestones. The white crosses at the US honour field in Margraten and the small white rectangle gravestones elsewhere are placed in tight neat rows in a green lawn. All military ranks are buried side by side, emphasising equality and brotherhood in death. The land is provided on loan from the Dutch government, and the cemeteries are managed by the Commonwealth War Graves Commission and the US Federal Government (Margraten). The cemeteries are frequently visited by relatives, foreign tourists and visitors.

In Bloemendaal, Noord-Holland, a special field of honour has been established for resistance fighters. A total of 347 men and women who were executed by the Germans during the war were reburied here after 1945. The honour field in Loenen, near Apeldoorn, was established in 1947 to bury the remains of the Dutch who had died in Germany. Today almost 4,000 people have been reburied here, and burials continue to take place on a regular basis. There are no straight rows of erected headstones at the cemetery, but simple plaques that are placed on both sides of meandering forest paths. Each grave represents its own story, showing the diversity of the victims of the Second World War. The cemetery in Loenen has a central chapel. Here a shrine can be found with memorial books with the names of all those who have been buried at the site. Also, there are some urns with the ashes of victims of the Nazi concentration camps. Since the 1980s soldiers and civilians who were killed during humanitarian and peace missions can also be (re)buried here.

9.2.4. German Military Cemetery Ysselsteyn

The largest war cemetery in the Netherlands can be found near the small village of Ysselsteyn, deliberately tucked away behind trees in an isolated area (Limburg). Nearly 32,000 German soldiers who died on Dutch soil are buried here, each with a grey concrete crosses inscribed with a name. The cemetery also is the final resting place of 550 stateless persons and Dutch quislings. The site was laid out in 1946, and chosen for its isolated location. There are no major roads or train stations in the area. The cemetery itself is completely surrounded by trees and hidden from sight. It is an uneasy memorial site that has been described as 'a place full of discomfort'.[8] The cemetery is managed by the German War Graves Foundation and is very much seen as an educational facility. German youngsters between the age of 14 and 16 are invited to help with the maintenance of the graves. During their stay they are confronted with the consequences of war.

In recent years, an increasing number of Dutch schools is showing interest in the cemetery. Historian Joost Roosendaal, together with his students at the Radboud University, has researched the personal stories behind the graves. They reveal who is actually buried at the cemetery and why. During the 2016 National Remembrance of the Dead, the National Broadcasting Company (NOS) discussed and showed an item on the Ysselsteyn Cemetery for the first time.[9] The

[8]Retrieved from http://www.trouw.nl/tr/nl/6700/Science/article/detail/4288263/2016/04/24/Een-kerkhof-vol-pieuze-ongemak.dhtml. Accessed on March 19, 2019.

[9]Retrieved from http://nos.nl/artikel/2103111-geef-weggestopte-duitse-begraafplaats-plek-in-onze-geschiedenis.html. Accessed on March 19, 2019.

increasingly open attitudes towards Ysselsteyn reflect the dynamic nature of the national commemorations. Because the generation that has directly experienced the war is gradually disappearing, the emphasis on education and prevention is increasing. The content and form of the commemorations must be given meaning for a new generation.

9.3. NOTABLE DEVELOPMENTS IN DUTCH MEMORIAL PRACTICES

9.3.1. Spontaneous Commemorations

The murders of politician Pim Fortuyn (2002), just days before the national elections, and the controversial filmmaker and publicist Theo van Gogh (2004), as well as the death of the popular singer André Hazes (2004), are ingrained in the collective memory of many Dutch. Unlike ordinary funerals, their memorial services were widely mediatised. The white coffin of André Hazes, positioned in the middle of the Amsterdam Arena during a farewell concert with 50,000 people, was broadcast live on National television. The funerals of Fortuyn and Van Gogh were not only mediatised, they were highly political. The applauding and rattling crowd at Fortuyn's funeral procession and the 'make-noise-demonstration' for Theo van Gogh were expressions of protest, a sign that outspoken people cannot be silenced through murder. In the case of Van Gogh, thousands of people gathered in Amsterdam to create noise with whistles, lids and pans instead of the usual silent and composed commemorative gatherings.

These new ways of public mourning both move and displease people. On the occasion of Fortuyn's funeral, writer and television producer Boudewijn Büch expressed his disgust in a spoken column on the television programme *Netwerk*:

> *Death does not deserve applause. Murder has no right to a flower homage. Mourning should not be accompanied by football songs. [...] For me death must remain dead; silent, sad and beyond imagination, dead still [...] I want to hear the birds whistling at the cemetery again. I do not want to hear the crackling of cellophane flower bouquets, the singing of hit parade songs and the chanting of slogans. I want death to return to what it ought to be: horrifying, incomprehensible and dreadful.*[10]

9.3.2. Dying Publicly

When René Gude was appointed 'Denker des Vaderlands' ('Thinker Laureate') in 2013, he was terminally ill.[11] He suffered from bone cancer, and his left leg had already been amputated. Being a philosopher, he wanted to approach his own imminent death with thought, reasoning and conversations: philosophy as 'humour management'. He continued to spread his visions on death and dying, and on life in general, through various popular media, and eventually passed away on 13 March 2015. In 2014, Gude published the booklet

---

[10] *Het carnaval der rouwenden* (The Carnival of Mourners) – see https://nederlands.nl/nedermap/verhalen/verhaal/35985.html?zoekresultaat=ja – was pronounced on 12 May 2002 in the news programme *Netwerk*: https://youtu.be/JkGxAR37rcM. Accessed on March 15, 2019.

[11] The honorary title 'Denker des Vaderlands' is an initiative of the 'Month of the Philosophy Association'/Stichting Maand van de Filosofie. For more information on René Gude, see https://isvw.nl/over-ons/rene-gude/. Accessed on March 14, 2019.

Dying Is Quite Simple. Anyone Can Do It in which he explains his views on dying and death in an interview with Wim Brands, a Dutch poet, journalist and TV presenter. Brands would die just a year later, when a short period of depression led to his unexpected suicide. At the time public discussion on dealings with suicide in the media were common, as the well-known writer Joost Zwagerman had died of suicide six months earlier. As happens often, the number of suicide attempts had spiked after Zwagerman's widely mediatised 'self-chosen' death.

Psychiatrist Jan Mokkenstorm, a pioneer in suicide prevention, therefore began to advise news programs on how to report on suicide in a more nuanced, conscious and life-saving way.[12] By describing suicide as a choice, Mokkenstorm argued, we strip it of its grim face. Although this might comfort the immediate family and close friends, it likely leads to new victims when presented to a general audience.[13] Contrary to the broad and detailed media attention that was paid to the suicide of Zwagerman, in the case of Wim Brands the cause of death was deliberately kept out of the headlines. In 2018, three years after Zwagerman's death and in celebration of his 55th birthday, a new documentary on his life and death was broadcasted, illustrating the grim face of suicide and the struggles of those left behind.[14] Dying has become an increasingly public event, as the cases of Gude, Brands and Zwagerman show.

---

[12]Retrieved from https://www.vn.nl/jan-mokkenstorm-wim-brands/. Accessed on March 16, 2019.

[13]Retrieved from https://www.113.nl/professionals-en-organisaties/media. Accessed on April 14, 2019.

[14]Verbraak, C. (2018). Retrieved from https://www.2doc.nl/documentaires/series/2doc/2018/november/joost-zwagerman.html

9.3.3. MH17: Public Mourning

Public death and mourning are seldom a model for the average death. Of the approximately 150,000 annual deaths in the Netherlands, only a few make the news. We either mourn exceptional people, like celebrities, or ordinary people who have died under exceptional circumstances. The public character of these deaths often instigates public discussions, for example about what is appropriate mourning and about the boundaries between public and private. In the Netherlands the MH17 disaster and the subsequent practice have set a new standard in public commemoration.

Malaysian Airlines flight MH17 on its way from Amsterdam to Kuala Lumpur was shot down on 17 July 2014 while flying over eastern Ukraine, killing all 283 passengers, the majority of whom were Dutch, and the 15 crew members on board. Their bodily remains were scattered over a wide and war-torn area, and could only be recovered at great effort and risk. A week later, on 23 July, the first bodily remains returned 'home' to the Netherlands. At this day, an official day of national mourning was declared. Church bells were ringing throughout the country when the first aircraft landed at Eindhoven airport. On board were 40 caskets, holding remains of the victims. After the *Last Post* was performed, public life came to a standstill and people observed a minute of silence.

Thousands of people witnessed on national television, how eight bearers, with great precision and care, carried 40 caskets one by one from the airplane to the hearses at Eindhoven airport. The careful placing of caskets in the cars took up most of the two-hour ceremony. Then a procession of 40 identical hearses made its way towards Hilversum, where the remains would be identified. Countless people had gathered along the 100-kilometre route to see the column of hearses and to pay their respects. Some threw flowers and watched in silence, whereas others greeted the procession with applause. Photos were taken to capture the moment. The ceremony at Eindhoven airport and the subsequent procession to Hilversum would be repeated eight more times over the weeks and months to come, in the exact same way and with the same ceremonial regard.[15]

That first ceremony on July 23 was part of a day of national mourning, a phenomenon the Dutch are not familiar with. The last time such a day was proclaimed was in 1962 with the death of Queen Wilhelmina, and in 1963 after the murder of American president Kennedy. Therefore, there was no protocol or living tradition to fall back on. A team of funeral directors successfully devised and organised the return ceremony in Eindhoven together with the help of the civil service and the military. A formal national commemoration ceremony was held on 10 November 2014 in the presence of 2,000 immediate family members and friends, the King and Queen, and members of Parliament. Since 2017 the annual commemoration takes place in a newly established memorial park in Vijfhuizen, near airport Schiphol, where 298 trees have been planted in memory of the victims.[16]

---

[15]23 July 2014: 40 caskets, 24 July: 74 caskets, 25 July: 75 caskets, 26 July: 38 caskets, 4 August: 1 casket, 8 November: 5 caskets, 28 November: 6 caskets, 7 February 2015: 1 casket and 1 May 2015: 7 caskets.

[16]For information on the memorial park, see http://www.monumentmh17.nl/

BIBLIOGRAPHY

Adams, A. & Schrauwen, A. (1992). *Ontwerpthema: Crematie*. Delft: Publikatieburo TU Delft.

Boon, R. (1987). De 'laatste eer' in gereformeerd-protestants milieu. Een geschiedenis van verwerping en eerherstel. *Eredienstvaardig*. 5 (3).

Brabers, J., Markx, S. & Reinders, W. (2006). *Uitvaartbegeleiding op humanistische grondslag*. Amsterdam: Humanistisch Verbond.

Bruin-Mollenhorst, J. & Hoondert, M. (2018). Musical media in Dutch crematoria, 1914–present. *Thanatos*. 1 (7), 2018.

Cappers, W. (1999). *Vuurproef voor een grondrecht. Koninklijke vereniging voor facultatieve crematie 1874–1999*. Zutphen: Walburg Pers.

Cappers, W. (2012). *Aan deze zijde van de dood. Funeraire componenten van seculariserende cultuurlandschappen in Nederland 1575–2010*. Arnhem.

Colenbrander, B.W. (1993). *Style: Standard and signature in Dutch architecture of the nineteenth and twentieth centuries*. Rotterdam: Nai Publishers.

Dienstboek, C. (1987). *Liturgie in dagen van rouw. Proeven voor de eredienst. Aflevering I*. Leidschendam, Leusden.

Congregation for the Doctrine of the Faith. (2016). *Instruction Ad resurgendum cum Christo regarding the burial of the deceased and the conservation of the ashes in the case of cremation*. Vatican City: Holy See Press Office.

Dessing, N. (2001). *Rituals of birth, circumcision, marriage and death among Muslims in the Netherlands*. Leuven: Peeters.

van Dijk, S. & Mennen, M.G. (2002). *Lijkbezorging in Nederland. Evaluatie Inspectierichtlijn, Overzicht van de Branche en Inzicht in Naleving van Regelgeving*. Bilthoven: RIVM.

Duijst-Heesters, W., Woudenberg-van den Broek, C. & Soerdjbalie-Maikoe, V. (2016). *De lijkschouw en sectie beschouwd. Een vergelijkend onderzoek naar systemen van lijkschouw en gerechtelijke sectie*. Den-Haag: Nederlands Forensisch Instituut, Ministerie van Veiligheid en Justitie.

Engelke, M. (2015). The coffin question: Death and materiality in humanist funerals. *Material Religion*. 1 (*11*), 26–48.

Franke, I. (1989). *Crematie in Nederland. 1875–1955*. Utrecht: Matrijs.

Gratama, S. (1888). Wet tot vaststelling van bepalingen betrekkelijk het begraven van lijken, de begraafplaatsen, en de begrafenisregten van den 10-den April 1869. *Staatsblad* no.65. 's-Gravengae. 75–76.

Heessels, M. (2012). *Bringing home the dead: Ritualizing cremation in the Netherlands*. Nijmegen: Radboud University.

Heessels, M., Poots, F. & Venbrux, E. (2012). In touch with the deceased: Animate objects and human ashes. *Material Religion*. 4 (*8*), 466–488.

Hekkema, H. (2002). Uitvaartcultuur als ontwerpopgave; De oesters zijn gegeten, de witte wijn is gedronken. In Hekkema, H. (ed.). *Uitvaartcultuur als ontwerpopgave: Situering en architectuur van funeraire functies in een veranderende samenleving; een ideeënprijsvraag voor studenten*. Zwolle: Esselink Stichting, 59–76.

Henselmans, M. (2017). *Laat je niet kisten door de commercie*. Oss: Genoeg.

Hoondert, M. & Arfman, W. (2013). Musicalising All Souls' Day rituals. *Yearbook for Ritual and Liturgical Studies*. (*29*), 113–131.

I&O Research. (2017). *Rapport Draagvlakonderzoek Resomeren. Rapportnummer 2017/028*.

Kadrouch Outmany, K. (2016). Religion at the cemetery Islamic burials in the Netherlands and Belgium. *Contemporary Islam*. 1 (*10*), 87–105.

Klaassens, M. & Groote, P. (2012). Designing a place for goodbye: The architecture of crematoria in the Netherlands. In D. Davies & C. Park (Eds.). *Emotion, identity and death: Mortality across disciplines*. Farnham: Ashgate.

Kok, H. (2005). *Thanatos. De geschiedenis van de laatste eer*. Heeswijk-Dinther: Berne Media.

LOB. (2017). *Veilig en gezond werken op begraafplaatsen: Arbo-richtlijnen in de praktijk 2007–2015*. Amsterdam: Landelijke Organisatie van Begraafplaatsen.

LOB. (2018). *Handboek Opgraven en Ruimen*. Amsterdam: Landelijke Organisatie van Begraafplaatsen.

de Maaker, E., Venbrux, E. & Quartier, T. (2011). Reinventing "All Souls' Day": Spirituality, contemporary art, and the remembrance of the dead. In A. Gregor (ed.). *Ritual dynamics and the science of ritual. Reflexivity, media and visuality* (pp. 617–634). Wiesbaden: Harrassowitz Verlag.

Martel, S. (2004). *Sterk als de dood. Sterven en rouw in joods perspectief*. Amsterdam: Eburon Uitgeverij.

Mathijssen, B. (2013). Pastors and relatives: Enacting Protestant and Catholic funeral liturgies in the Netherlands. In E. Venbrux, T. Quartier, C. Venhorst, and B. Mathijssen (Eds.). *Changing European death ways*. Münster: Lit Verlag, 213–239.

Mathijssen, B. (2017a). *Making sense of death. Ritual practices and situational beliefs of the recently bereaved in the Netherlands*. Münster: Lit Verlag.

Mathijssen, B. (2017b). The ambiguity of human ashes: Exploring encounters with cremated remains in the Netherlands. *Death Studies*. 1 (*41*), 34–41.

Multatuli. (1952). *Volledige werken IV. Een en ander over Pruisen en Nederland. Causerieën. De maatschappij tot nut van den Javaan. Ideeën, derde bundel*. Amsterdam: van Oorschot, 717.

Nationale Raad voor Liturgie. (1976). *Liturgie van de sacramenten en andere kerkelijke vieringen. De Uitvaartliturgie*. Hilversum: Gooi & Sticht.

Nissen, P. (2013). Words for the final hour. On deathbed prayer in the Christian tradition. In E. Venbrux, T. Quartier, C. Venhorst, and B. Mathijssen (Eds.). *Changing European death ways*. Münster: Lit Verlag.

Obdeijn, H. & Schrover, M. (2008). *Komen en gaan. Immigratie en emigratie in Nederland vanaf 1550*. Amsterdam: Uitgeverij Bert Bakker.

Oberman, H. (2003). *The two reformations. The journey from the last days to the new world.* New Haven, CT: Yale University Press.

Parry, J.P. (1994). *Death in Banaras.* Cambridge: Cambridge University Press.

Peelen, J. (2012). Tussen leven en dood. Rituelen rondom zwangerschapsverlies in Nederland. *Yearbook for Ritual and Liturgical Studies.* (*28*), 259–265.

Peelen, J. (2012). *Between birth and death. Rituals of pregnancy loss in the Netherlands.* Nijmegen: Radboud University.

Quartier, T. (2007). *Bridging the gaps. An empirical study of Catholic funeral rites.* Münster: Lit Verlag.

Raak, C. (1995). *Dodenakkers.* Amsterdam: Arbeiderspers.

Sinnema, D., Moser, C. & Selderhuis, H. (Eds.). (2014). *Acta et Documenta Synodi Nationalis Dordrechtanae (1618–1619).* Göttingen: Vandenhoeck & Ruprecht.

Schmeets, H. (2016). *De religieuze kaart van Nederland, 2010–2015.* Den-Haag: Centraal Bureau voor de Statistiek.

Spruit, R. (1986). *De dood onder ogen.* Houten: De Haan.

Stoffels, H. & Walinga, P. (2005). Ontwikkelingen in de ledenaantallen van een aantal Nederlandse kerkgenootschappen (tabel). In SCP (ed.). *De sociale staat van Nederland.* Den Haag: Sociaal en Cultureel Planbureau.

Swhajor, A., Heessels, M., Van der Velde, P. & Venbrux, E. (2010). Aan de Ganges in Twente. Onderhandelen over vormgeven van hindoe-dodenrituelen in Nederland. *Quotidian. Dutch Journal for the Study of Everyday Life.* (2), 83–102.

TNO-Rapport. (2018). *Veiligheidsanalyse Resomeren. TNO 2018 R10677.*

TU Delft. (2018). *Beoordelingskader Alternatieve Vormen van Lijkbezorging*. Delft: Design for Values Institute.

Turner, V. (1969). *The ritual process. Structure and anti-structure*. Ithaca: Cornell University Press.

UitvaartBranchemonitor. (2018). *Stand van de uitvaartbranche 2017*. Den Haag: Uitvaartmedia.

Van den Broeke, L. (2015). No funeral sermons: Dutch or Calvinistic prohibition?. In T. Rasmussen & J. Øygarden Flæten (Eds.). *Preparing for death, remembering the dead* (pp. 361–377). Göttingen: Vandenhoeck & Ruprecht.

Van der Pijl, Y. (2007). *Levende-doden. Afrikaans-Surinaamse percepties, praktijken en rituelen rondom dood en rouw*, Bronnen voor de studie van Suriname, deel 27. Amsterdam: IBS, Rozenberg Publishers.

Van der Pijl, Y. (2017). The birth of a multicultural funeral home. *Death Studies*. 1 (*41*), 42–50.

Van der Ven, J. (2013). On the brink of death. Euthanasia from the angle of law, morality and religion: A cross-cultural perspective. In E. Venbrux, T. Quartier, C. Venhorst, and B. Mathijssen (Eds.). *Changing European Death Ways*. Münster: Lit Verlag.

Van Deutekom, H. & Van de Beek, K. (2017). *Gemeentelijke uitvaarten. Ontwikkelingen in 2016*. Ede: Christelijke Hogeschool Ede.

Venbrux, E., Heessels, M. & Bolt, S. (Eds.). (2008). *Rituele creativiteit: actuele veranderingen in de uitvaart- en rouwcultuur in Nederland*. Zoetermeer: Meinema.

Venbrux, E., Peelen J. & Altena M. (2009). Going Dutch: Individualisation, secularisation and changes in death rites. *Mortality*. 2 (*14*), 97–101.

Venbrux, E., Quartier, T., Venhorst, C. & Mathijssen, B. (Eds.). (2013). *Changing European death ways*. Münster: Lit Verlag.

Venhorst, C. (2013). *Muslims ritualising death in the Netherlands. Death rites in a small-town context*. Münster: Lit Verlag.

Venhorst, C. & Mathijssen, B. (2017). *Dood. Wegwijs in de Nederlandse Uitvaartcultuur*. Almere: Parthenon.

Vereeniging voor Facultatieve Lijkverbranding. (1877). *Berichten en mededelingen 1875–1955*, (1), 21–22. 's-Gravenhage.

Warnaar, M., Stoof, R. & Schonewille, G. (2017). *Kennis en bewustzijn van uitvaartkosten*. Utrecht: Nibud.

Wojtkowiak, J., Rutjens, B. & Venbrux, E. (2010). Meaning making and death in a secular society: A Dutch survey study. *Archive for the Psychology of Religion*. (*32*), 363–373.

Wouters, C. (2002). The quest for new rituals in dying and mourning: Changes in the we-I balance. *Body & Society*. 1 (*8*), 1–2.

INDEX

A-statement, 163
Advertising, 54
Aefferden, Josephine van, 141–142
Alkaline hydrolysis, 35–36
All Souls' Day, 188–190, 191–196
Amsterdam, 1–2, 19–20, 40–41, 52–53, 73, 82–83, 142–144, 153–155, 160–162, 172–173, 192–193, 196, 199
Anonymous death, 125–126
Apeldoorn Funeral Society, 40–41
Apeldoornsche Begrafenisvereeniging, 40–41
Après la Vie Academie, 47
Ar-Raza, Almere, 118–119
Arbeiders Vereeniging voor Lijkverbranding (AVVL), 17–19, 40–41, 155–156
Arbowet. *See* Working Conditions Legislation
Architecture, 160–162
Archive of Stones, 117–118, 134
Ardanta, 44–45
Arnhem, 53
Artists, 181, 183
Arya Samaadj, 83
Ashes. *See* Cremated remains
Ashes jewellery, 38, 180–181
Ashes, retrieval of, 178–180
Assisted suicide, 25–26, 28
Association for Entrepreneurs in the Funeral World (VOU), 45
Association of Non-Profit Funeral Societies (LSUW), 45–46
Association to Introduce Cremation in the Netherlands, 17–19, 152–153, 156

Auditorium, 168–170
Auschwitz Committee Netherlands, 192–193
Autopsy. *See* Cause of death

B-statement, 163
Basisregistratie Personen (BRP), 36–37
Bergerbos, natural burial, 108, 112, 119–122, 132–133
Besluit op de Lijkbezorging. See Corpse Disposal Act
Bier, 91, 99
Bloemendaal military cemetery, 194
Blogs, 191
BRANA, 121
Brancheblad Uitvaartzorg, 45
Branchevereniging Gecertificeerde Nederlandse Uitvaartondernemingen (BGNU), 45
Brands, architect, 143–144
Brands, Wim, 197–198
Büch, Boudewijn, 196–197
Burial, 11–12, 16, 26, 29–31, 58–59, 74, 98–99, 105, 157–159
  ashes, 194
  authorities, 58
  in churches, 11–12, 13–16, 105
  clearance, 130
  definition, 28
  fees, 132–133
  groundwater, 1–2, 108, 127
  grounds, 106–107, 108, 111, 112, 119–120, 128, 132–133, 142–143
  insurance, 59–61
  numbers of, 107, 108–109, 147–148
  pressure on space, 1–2, 15
  soil, 121
  types, 109
Burial Act 1869, 105–106, 109, 153, 156, 162–164

Calvinism, 9–10
  and burial, 11–12, 138
  and cremation, 10–12
  and history, 9–10
  in the Netherlands, 9–11
Calvinist funerary practices, 10–12
Calvinist members, 10–11
Cancer, 24
Caribbean, 1, 74
Catafalque, 99, 169–170
Catholic Church, 19
  and consecration, 112–113
  and cremation, 19
  history, 9–10
  and members, 157
  in the Netherlands, 81, 113–115

Catholic funeral liturgy, 81, 95
Cause of death, 13–15, 25–26, 28, 69, 94, 163, 198
Cemeteries, 105
- Amsterdam, 142
- architecture, 132–133, 160–162
- Beth Haim, 117–118, 144–145
- chapels, 16–17, 105, 111
- children, 65, 188
- clearing, 130
- closing, 31
- De Nieuwe Ooster, 142–144
- Dwingeloo, 117–118
- Glanerbrug, 146–147
- governance, 193–194
- Groningen, 131–132
- landscaping, 132–133
- layout, 127
- legalities, 29, 30
- maintenance, 17–19, 153
- management, 109–111, 129, 132–134, 135–137
- Marken, 138, 140
- Muiderberg, 82–83
- municipal, 30, 108, 109, 111, 113–115, 131–132, 135–137, 147–148
- natural, 121
- Oude Oosterbegraafplaats, 142
- Ouderkerk aan de Amstel, 82–83, 117–118, 143–144
- overcrowding, 107
- ownership, 151–152
- pet, 123–125
- pillarisation, 2–3
- Roermond, 140–142
- sections within, 16–17
- Sint Michelsgestel, 148–149
- special, 30–31, 112–125
- stillborn, 65, 188
- Syrian Orthodox, 146–147
- Usselo, 183–184
- Volendam, 138–140
- War, 122–123, 193–194

Centraal Bureau voor de Statistiek, 6, 23
Certificate of Death, 28, 59, 65
Charging the cremator, 98, 171–172, 174
Charitable donations at funerals, 78
Chevra Kadisha, 82–83
Children
- funeral costs, 65
- graves, 138–140, 142
- legislation, 36–37

Christian theology, 112–113
Christianity in the Netherlands, 6
Church community, 80–81
- *See also* Parish

Churchyards. *See* Special cemeteries
Celebrants, 58–59, 78
Clearing graves, 108–109, 130, 153
Code Pénal, 13–15
  See also Napoleonic Code
Coffin, 28, 30, 77–78, 88–89, 99, 127, 171, 174, 177–178
  bearers, 99
  biodegradable, 30, 75–76
  costs, 77
  and cremation service, 98
  and shroud, 75–77
Columbaria, 127–128
Commemoration, 195–196
  cemetery, 187
  holocaust, 191–196
  at home, 187
  MH17, 199–200
  plaques, 194
  virtual, 190–191
  war, 191–196
Commercials, 54–56
Committal, 98–99
Commonwealth War Graves Commission, 193–194
Congregation for the Doctrine of the Faith, 115
Consensus decision making. *See* *Poldermodel*
Conservation, 86
Continuing bonds, 115–116
Cooperation, 156
Coroner, 25–26, 28, 69
Corpse Disposal Act 1955, 26–34, 107, 156–157, 162–164
Corpse Disposal Act 1991, 20–21, 122, 125–126, 180–181
Cortege, 89–90, 91
Covering, 127, 129, 134, 177–178
  See also Coffin
Cremated remains, 71, 115, 163–164, 166–167, 174–175, 178, 180–181
  and commemoration, 188
  and Hinduism, 183–184
  at home, 180–181
  and modes of disposal, 115
  in public places, 199
  and Protestantism, 121
  and Roman Catholicism, 115
Cremation, 17–19, 28, 31–32, 98–99, 151
  certification, 162–166
  costs, 58–59
  and emancipation movement, 17–19
  environment, 38
  first, 17–19, 153–156, 174
  history, 17–19
  legalisation, 34–35, 159
  number of, 107, 159, 160
  process, 174–175
  propaganda, 156

services, 159, 166–167, 168–170
technical, 59–61, 63, 64–65, 174–175
waiting period, 34–35, 164
Cremator room, 98, 166–167, 171–173, 178
Crematoria, 19–20, 31, 38, 58–59, 76–77, 78, 99–100, 123–125, 151, 171
architecture, 160–162
auditoriums, 168–170
governance, 156–157
legislation, 26–27, 164
logistics, 166–178
management, 129, 132–134, 135–137
municipal, 31
numbers of, 19, 157
ownership, 152
private, 159
staffing, 132–133
time slots, 168–169
Cremulation, 178
Creole, 44, 87
Cryomeren, 35–36

De Nieuwe Ooster, 142–144, 160–162, 172–173
De Vereeniging tot Invoering der Lijkverbranding in Nederland, 17–19, 152–153
Dead bodies
care of, 33, 84–89
dressing, 85
embalming, 86
Muslim, 85, 97
ritual washing, 82, 85, 87, 97
thanatopraxy, 86, 88–89
transport, 75–76, 89–90
viewing, 87–89
washing, 85–86, 87
Death, 11–12, 23–24, 68–70, 187
causes of, 24
notices, 75
number of, 23–24, 108–109
place of, 24, 68
registration, 13–15
Deathbed, 10–11, 68–69, 83
Dekker, Eduard Douwes. *See* Multatuli
DELA, 38, 40–41, 44–45, 53, 55
Demographic context, 23
Digital recording, 99–100
Dinariwroko, 87
Direct cremation. *See* Technical cremation
Diversity, 3–6
Do-it-yourself funerals, 52
Docendo, 47
Dodenbussen, 13
Dodenherdenking, 19–20, 191–192
Donation, 78
Dordrecht Synod, 10–11

Dr C.J. Vaillant, 153–155, 184–185
Driehuis, 153–155, 159–162
Droog, Bart FM, 73
Dutch Association of Approved Funeral Entrepreneurs (NUVU), 45
Dutch Association of Certified Dutch Funeral Enterprises (BGNU), 45
Dutch Reformed Church, 9–11, 81, 115–116, 157
Dutch Republic, 10
Dutch Revolt, 9–10

Eastern Orthodox Church (Syrian), 146–147
Education, 47–48
Eighteenth century, 12–17
Eighty Years' War, 9–10
Eindhoven, 40–41, 53, 199–200
Embalming, 86
  prohibition on, 33
  repatriation, 33
  royal family, 86
Enlightenment, 13
Environmental concerns, 160–162
Eucharist, 96
Euthanasia, 20–21, 24–26
Exhumation, 30, 130, 144

Facebook, 54–55, 190–191
Facultatieve, 156, 160–162
Family graves, 140–141
Fields of honour, 193–194
Flowers, 77–78
Fock, minister, 152–153
Foetus, 65
Fortuyn, Pim, 196
Foundation for Funeral Care Examinations (Stivu), 47
Foundation Quality Mark Funeral Care (SKU), 47–48
Franchise, 44–45
Funeral
  associations, 42–43, 52
  attendance at, 13–15
  attire, 16
  charitable donations, 78
  Christian, 74, 80–81, 91, 95–96
  coffee-table, 79, 103, 171
  combined, 59–61
  cooperatives, 43–44
  costs, 12–13
  digital recording, 99–100
  directors, 44, 47–49, 50–51, 52, 61–62, 87, 133–134, 200
  do-it-yourself, 52
  endowment, 59–61
  foundations, 42–43
  funds, guilds, 42–43
  industry, 34–36, 38, 46, 51–52

history, 39–41
in-kind, 59–62
insurance, 39, 43–45, 59–62, 70, 75, 77
insurers, 44–45, 54, 72–73
making arrangements, 49, 70–74
museum Tot Zover, 144
music, 78, 171
Muslim, 44
non-ecclesial, 97–98
notices, 75
personal, 50–51
poverty, 62–63
prayer, 82, 97
secular, 100
tailor-made, 20–21, 67–68, 94
trade associations, 45–46
training and qualifications, 47
Funeral Act. *See* Corpse Disposal Act

GaandeweG Uitvaart Educatie, 47
Gardens of Remembrance, 188
Gemeentewege. *See* Municipality
Gender, 50–53
General Synod of the Reformed Churches, 157
Generality Lands, 10
Gereformeerde Kerk, 10
German War Graves Foundation, 195
Ghusl, 87
Goeie Mie. *See* Swanenburg, Maria Catharina
Grashoek, 123–125
Grave, 125–137
backfilling, 99
clearing, 109, 130
depth, 127
digging, 127–128
dimensions, 128
general, 29, 125–126, 130, 132–133, 138–140, 143–144
Islamic, 118–119
Jewish, 117–118
lease, 143
objects, 99, 116, 121–122, 135
private, 29–30, 126–127, 129–130, 131–132, 138
Protestant, 115–116
renewal fee, 129
rights, 129–130
Roman Catholic, 112–115
terms, 129–130
types, 109, 125–126
visiting, 116
with the hands, 141–142
Grebbeberg Military Cemetery, 122–123
Green burial. *See* Natural burial

Green cremation. *See* Resomation
Groesbeek, 193–194
Gude, René, 197–198
Guilds, 12–13, 39–40, 42–43

Hazes, André, 196
Hearses, 199–200
Health Council of the Netherlands, 35–36
Heritage, 50–53
Heritage reallocation, 53
Hervormde Kerk, 9–10
Hindu, 83, 183–184
  ash scattering, 183–184
  priests. *See* Pandit
Holocaust, 144, 191–193
Holocaust Names Memorial, 192–193
Holy Roman Emperor Joseph II, 13–15
Hospitals, 48, 84–85, 189–190
House of Parliament, 34–35
House of Representatives, 26–27, 156
Humanist, 74
Humanist Association, 83–84
Humanistic celebrant, 83–84

Identification stone, 163–164, 174
Imam, 81–82
Independent Islamic cemetery, 118–119
Internet and funerary practice, 190–191
Islam, 148–149
Islamic cemeteries, 118–119
Islamic funerary practice, 68–69

Javanese, 74, 148–149
Jewish, 117–118
  burial society, *Joods begrafeniswezen*, 82–83
  cemeteries, 117–118
  funerary practice, 68–69
  hospice, 82–83
Judaism, 82–83
Jurisprudence, 37–38

Karres, architect, 143–144
King Willem I, 15
Koninklijke Facultatieve. *See* Association to Introduce Cremation in the Netherlands
KRO (Katholieke Radio Omroep), 188–189
Kuyper, Abraham, 9–10

Labour workers, 38
Law, 30–31
  on burial, 15–16, 17–19
  on cremation, 162–166
  on euthanasia, 25–26
Lijkschouwing, 69
Liturgical formats, 95

Live-streaming funeral services, 99–100
Local authorities, 58, 62, 63, 72–73, 108, 159, 162–163
See also Municipality
Local Plans, 31, 108
Loenen Field of Honour, 122–123
Lonely death, 73–74
Lonely Funeral Association, 73

Margraten, 193–194
Mariënhage convent, 53
Marken, 138–140
Marketing, 51–52
Mass, 135
Meander, 47
Medical certificate of the cause of death, 28, 59, 65
Medical practitioner, 69
Medicalisation, 20–21
Memorial services, 73–74, 94–95, 196
Memorials, 77–78, 103, 133–134, 145, 188
at cemeteries, 187
and removal, 31
and war, 122–123
Metropolis, 2
MH17, 199–200
memorial park, 200
Migration, 3–6
Military cemetery, 122–123
Minister, 11–12, 16, 34–35, 80–81
Mokkenstorm, Jan, 198
Monuments. *See* Memorials
Monuta, 40–41, 44–45, 54–55, 131–132
Mortality rates, 23–24
Mortuary, 45, 84–85
technicians, 48–49, 50–51, 84–85, 86
Mourning
attire, 16, 19–20
cards, 58–59, 75, 93–94
room, 49–50, 53, 77, 87–88, 168
Muis, Albert, 143–144
Multatuli, 153–155
Multicultural, 20–21
Municipal cemetery, 30–31, 108, 109, 111, 113–115, 131–132, 138, 147–148
Municipal funeral services, 63
Municipality, 1, 15–16, 29–30, 31, 71, 72–73, 109–111
Music, 78, 171
Muslim, 6, 52, 68–69, 74, 79–80, 82, 87, 118–119, 147–148
burial, 111, 118, 147–149
funerary practice, 81–82, 97
Moroccan, 81–82
Surinamese Javanese, 148–149
Turkish, 147–148

Napoleonic Code, 13–15
NARDUS Cooperative Funeral Organisations, 45–46
National Day of Mourning, 19–20
National Remembrance of the Dead, 19–20, 191–192
Natural burial, 119–120, 121–122, 143–144
  ground pets, 123–125
  grounds, 108, 112, 119–122, 123–125, 132–133
Natuurmonumenten Nederland, 119–120
Nederlandse Vereniging van Erkende Uitvaartondernemers (NUVU), 45
Netherlands statistics. *See* Centraal Bureau voor de Statistiek
NHA, 47
Nibud, 57–58, 63–65
NIK, 117–118
Nineteenth century, 2–3, 4–5, 9–10, 106, 107, 109, 116, 164
Nuvema, 44–45
Nuyten, H.C.P., 160–162
Ode aan de doden, 188–189
Oosterbeek, 193–194
Orders of service, 93
Organisation of Jewish Communities in the Netherlands (NIK), 117–118
Orthodox Church Syrian cemetery, 146–147
OrthoMetals, 184–185

Pandit, 83
Parish governance, 112–115
Pastor, 80–81
Perpetuity, 118–119, 121
Personal Records Database Act (BRP), 36–37, 65
Personalised funerary practices, 64–65, 78
Pet cemetery, 123–125
Photographs, 100, 121–122
Pillarisation, 2–3
Planning, 31, 72–73
Plots, 111, 113–115, 147–149
Poel, Marius, 160–162
Poldermodel, 3
Population, 2, 6, 15, 23–24, 35–36, 52–53, 153
Post-mortem care, 28, 62, 69, 84–85

Poverty, 62–63
Prayer cards, 100–102
Prayers for the death, 16, 81–82, 97, 99
Pre-paid funeral plans. *See* Funeral insurance
Price comparison websites, 57–58, 78, 190–191
Priest, 80–81
Protestant
  cemeteries, 116
  Church in the Netherlands, 6, 11–12, 16, 19, 95, 96, 115–116
  funerary practices, 10–12, 16–17, 80, 95, 96, 140
  graves, 116
Protestant Reformation, 115–116
Protestantism. *See* Calvinism

Quality Mark Funeral Care, 47–48

Randstad, 2, 108, 131–133
Redevelopment, 143–144
Reformation, 10–11
Reformed Churches in the Netherlands, 81, 116, 157
Religious Affiliation, 8
Religious belief and funerary practice, 85
Remembrance cards, 100–102
Remembrance public, 187
Repatriation, 97, 164
Resomation, 35–36
Ritual, 50–51, 81, 82, 84
  coaches, 80–81, 84
  washing, 82, 85, 87, 97
Royal family, 34, 86, 192

Ṣalāt al-Janāzah, 97
Salvation, 115–116
Samenwerkingsverband van Uitvaartverenigingen zonder Winstoogmerk (LSUW), 45–46
Sanatan Dharm, 83
Section, 31, 32
Secularity, 95, 100
Segregation, 2–3
Senate, 24–25, 36–37
Servo Elieser, 145
Seventeenth century, 9–12
Shroud burial, 20–21, 75–77
Sixteenth century, 9–12
Slavery, commemoration of, 145
Special cemeteries, 30–31, 112–125
Special Income Support, 63–64
Springer, architect, 142
Stichting De Eenzame Uitvaart, 73

Stichting Keurmerk Uitvaartzorg (SKU), 47–48
Stichting Vakexamens Uitvaartzorg (Stivu), 47
Stillbirth, 65, 163, 191
Suicide, 25–26, 28, 197–198
Surinam, 5, 83, 145
Sustainability, 35–36
Swanenburg, Maria Catharina, 164

Taboo, 54
Tahara,, 87
Tailor-made funerary practices, 20–21, 67–68, 94
Technical cremation, 59–61, 63, 64–65, 174–175
Television, 3, 54–55, 192, 196–197
Termination of life on request. *See* Euthanasia
Thanatopraxy, 45, 86, 88–89

Urbanisation, 15, 48, 106–107, 153
US Federal Government, 193–194

Van der Lee, Ida, 188–189
Van Gogh, Theo, 196
Vereniging voor Ondernemers in de Uitvaartwereld (VOU), 45
Volunteers, 42–43, 48–49, 73–74, 81–83, 132–133

Wake, 77, 87–88
War
  cemeteries, 106–107, 122–123, 193–194, 195
  memorial, 122–123
Wasi dede, 87
Water, 1–2, 35–36, 119–120, 138–140, 143–144, 183–184
Wegerif, A.H., 160–162
Welfare State, 1–2
Wereldlichtjesdag, 189–190
Westerhoff, 152
Wet op de lijkbezorging. *See* Corpse Disposal Act
Wils, Jan, 160–162
Witnessing the charge, 172–173
Women, 50–52, 82
Workers Association for Cremation (AVVL), 17–19, 40–41, 155–156
Working Conditions Legislation, 38, 130

World War, First, 3, 17–19, 40–41, 122–123
World War, Second, 2–3, 17, 19–20, 106–107, 122–123, 140–141, 143, 156–157, 192, 194
Worldwide Candle Lighting Day, 189–190
Yarden, 40–41, 44–45, 52–53, 55–56, 160–162
Yardenhuis Amsterdam, 160–162
YouTube, 85, 191
Ysselsteyn military cemetery, 195–196

Zwagerman, Joost, 197–198

www.ingramcontent.com/pod-product-compliance
Lightning Source LLC
LaVergne TN
LVHW022203200926
848481LV00006B/1831